MW01180987

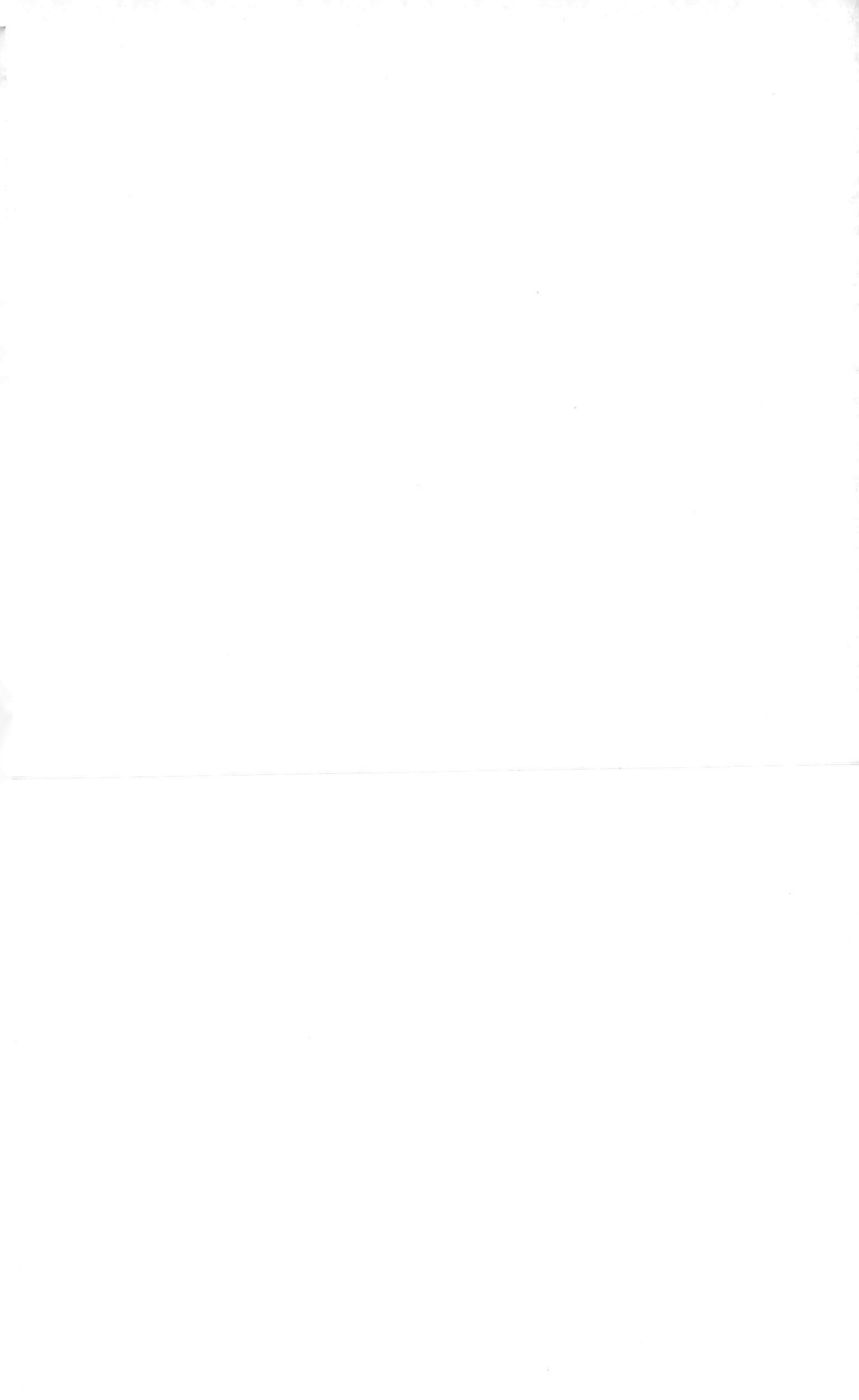

Why Aren't You Listening to Me?

Elevate Your Emotional Intelligence and Connect With Your Team

TERESA LODATO, CPCC

Balboa Press books may be ordered through booksellers or by contacting:

Balboa Press
A Division of Hay House
1663 Liberty Drive
Bloomington, IN 47403
www.balboapress.com
1 (877) 407-4847

Print information available on the last page.

ISBN: 978-1-9822-4207-7 (sc)
ISBN: 978-1-9822-4206-0 (hc)
ISBN: 978-1-9822-4208-4 (e)

Library of Congress Control Number: 2020901565

Balboa Press rev. date: 01/30/2020

Dedicated to my Rock,
whose superior communication skills and
willingness to listen to his heart
became the reason we are together,
&
To our three children, may you listen and learn to succeed
in life, creating a better world in which to live.

Table of Contents

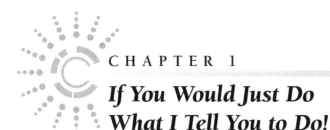

CHAPTER 1
If You Would Just Do What I Tell You to Do!

"She was never prepared for half the shit she went through, but she got through it. She always will."
– Abby Rose

"Frustrating."

That is the answer my client Lauren Anderson gives me when I ask how things are going. She is thirty-eight years old and lives with her husband and two children in Ocean Colony, a gated community located in Half Moon Bay, California. She is a very driven individual and has experienced the success that comes from hard work, discipline, and focus. Her thick, brown hair falls smoothly along her face. Her blunt cut makes her look serious and professional, which I imagine is intentional. Her home is stunningly beautiful at over 4,500 square feet and overlooking the Pacific Ocean. "I have made it" seems to be what everything is screaming to me.

As I wait for Lauren to answer more, I wonder what I could do for her that she is not able to do for herself. This one will be interesting, I muse.

"Why don't you start off telling me a little about yourself? I'm curious to hear about what has brought you to coaching."

Lauren looks at her watch a bit irritated and then sighs.

"I started out at Merrill as a financial advisor where I quickly became a top producer. 'Being a financial advisor is not that difficult of a job, so long as you do what you are told to do, are disciplined in your work and stay in integrity…' That's what my district manager told me when I was hired. I listened to him, put my nose to the grindstone and have worked my ass off over the past fifteen years. I was a great financial advisor, my clients counted on me to create portfolios to get them to their goals. They listened to what I said and did everything I recommended to them. Together, we made a lot of money. I remember my boss telling me that you attract clients that are just like you. It was so true. It was wonderful getting results and winning club year after year. I certainly had what it took to get the job done! Because I am so successful at my job, I was asked to open a new office here in Half Moon Bay which has been doing incredibly well. I handpicked the advisors working with me and the results we have been turning in is what resulted in my promotion to district manager. Although I have always enjoyed the work I do, the results I get and the perks of being a top producer, I am really struggling with work relationships now that I run the district. Everything feels like an uphill battle and managing so many people is making me long for just being able to deal with my clients and home office advisors who are all like me. Back then, I knew exactly how to get results, and everyone benefited from my advice. Now only about 25 percent of the financial advisors are listening to me, so I am not getting the results I need and corporate is breathing down my neck. My manager says I need to figure out how to work with different personalities, but I think people just need to do what I am telling them to do. After all, they made me manager because I get results, so I know how to get things done! I have also been suffering from really bad headaches, but I just keep popping Excedrin and pushing through. The job has to get done and I am the only one who can do it, you know?"

I smile and take a deep breath.

"So, tell me what you would like to receive coaching on today?"

She continues, "I'm getting worried that I might lose my job and I would have to start all over again building a book of clients at another firm. I just don't know if I have it in me to do that, since it took an incredible amount of time when I began and now, I've got kids…." Her voice trails off and her face looks pained at the idea of starting over.

"Hmmm, that is a great place to start. Let's break this down a bit so we can get really clear about what is going on for you. Right now, you still have your job, correct?"

Lauren nods her head yes.

"Okay, so how about we focus on just the thought of possibly losing your job. We will leave thoughts of starting over for another time."

I watch as Lauren's shoulders drop slightly, and she lets go a small sigh of relief. I imagine she is comforted that we have a structure in place, are dividing and conquering her problem and seem to be cutting directly to the chase.

"Before we get to that however, I am curious to know where else your work challenges are showing up in your life."

Lauren stiffens and I know we are getting to the reason she called me.

"All this stress I am experiencing is having a horrible impact on my family too. My normally loving and easy-going husband is growing distant, and even my children don't seem to like me very much anymore. I am stressed out all the time, my back hurts and these bad headaches feel like my head is on an anvil and the blacksmith is hammering away. Although I am thirty-eight, I feel closer to sixty. I am struggling in all areas of my life and I just need it to stop! If everyone would just listen to me and do as they are told, everything could go back to the way things used to be!".

Can you relate to Lauren's story? Are you frustrated that meetings take so long because your team members and employees spend so much time talking about what is going on instead of making progress on projects, going off half-cocked with ideas that have no proven success, or worse want to spend far too much time researching every detail? Do you long for the days when it was just you at your job, or when your team was made up of people just like you? People whose only goal is to get results? You are not alone, and there is nothing wrong with you.

Lauren's type is leader. She is driven, focused on the outcome, attentive to the task at hand. She is action-oriented and speaks with confidence and authority. She is not interested in small talk but insists rather to get straight to the point. My years of working and living with these fierce and competent individuals have taught me that we need people like this in our world. The action takers, task conquerors, and highly result-driven clients I coach have much going for them, but they (like everyone) have some aspects that are not so great. This is where I come in, my ability to speak with anyone stems from my curiosity about them, their life and passions, and this is what I teach my clients to do as well: talk so people will listen, and listen so people feel heard. From there you can begin to develop relationships that are supportive and collaborative. But we will get there a little later. Right now, we have some fun things to explore, namely getting to know you.

One of the struggles I often hear from my clients is that they are doing a lot of work and putting forth a great deal of effort, but do not seem to be getting the results that they want or are accustomed to getting. In addition, they are experiencing chronic health challenges and an intermittent personal life. They are very professional and are not much for small talk, preferring instead to get right to work and communicate in a way that is brief and to the point, so they often get frustrated with other people who do not observe their to-the-point business style. Sigh. Not only can business relationships suffer, but often my clients struggle in their personal relationships as well. They experience relationships with people who challenge them constantly, who are too wishy washy, or worse, spend too long to make a decision because they have to research every. little. thing.

Here are five things I want you to know as we begin:

1. Every person has masculine and feminine qualities within them. Learning how to balance these aspects is what will lead you to experience more ease and get better results with less effort.
2. The way you communicate, from the words you choose, the intonation in your voice and your body language, are all critical to getting buy-in from people around you.
3. Being successful with various forms of communication that compel the people around you to move into action is a skill that you can learn and will benefit you in all areas of your life.
4. There *is* a way to embrace your amazing ability to get things done without offending people around you and it begins with the relationship to yourself.
5. You are not a human doing, but rather a human *being*. Remember the reason you are here.

In getting to know yourself and being true to your innate nature, you experience fulfillment. If you are not experiencing a deep sense of fulfillment in your life, it is an indicator that you are not fully in relationship with yourself at a core level. You could be trying too hard to do things the way you are *supposed to,* that you *want them* to happen, rather than the other way around. Most people start with what they want on an external level, expecting change to happen to their situation or to others. But as the Dalai Lama says, "Be the change you want to see in the world," this book will show you exactly how to do just that. One of the best things that happens when you flip the paradigm you are living, is that you begin trusting yourself. Rather than living your life the way you were *told to* live it or experiencing multiple failures because you didn't have good models for easeful success in life, you become clear, naturally more secure and confident. When you understand yourself and can see where tweaks can be made, you create a plan for success and are able to fully relax into each moment. Being fully relaxed allows your body to heal and regenerate much like when a video game avatar uses a health pack to power up its life or health gauge when it is low. Persistent seeking of the truth is what leads to self-discovery, which leads to improved health, healthier relationships, and more productivity with better results. You burn yourself out when you are not fully in alignment with yourself. You experience missed work and school, miss out on time with family and friends, experience lack and limitations in life as if you are hitting walls. In addition, lack refers to your inability to manifest and experience abundance as well. The healthiest and most successful way to live is by creating a balanced life. When you are centered and clear, you are in alignment with your best self, and from this point you create and project your desires for what is possible into your future. When you are not clear, your essence is weaker and brings unwanted consequences in your life. Your body is an incredible complex system with so much wisdom and knowledge literally embedded in your DNA. Your body is a human recording device which programs your autonomic systems and creates the framework for how your life plays out. Your body is the antennae which sends out signals; it is the set production artist and writer that set the scene in the theater which is your life. Therefore, it is critical that you pay attention to the systems in place and change the ones that no longer help you reach your goals and live a life that is aligned with who and where you aim to be.

You are an individual and yet are also one united being at the core of your essence. Much like water when poured into different containers takes on the unique shape of the container, we too are of one essence poured into different vessels in order to serve our purpose in life. You have unique tools and gifts much like the special powers attributed to a superhero. Additionally, uncovering your gifts helps you to understand and accomplish your purpose in this lifetime. Being centered and aware changes the manner in which you communicate and like changing the manner in which a water nozzle sprays, you can create a soft or forceful flow in your relationships. This ability to change and adapt to your environment is your greatest ally and life skill you can utilize. Since no one knows all the answers all of the time, you can take comfort in knowing that you have your own personal Google within your body as it is giving you signals all the time to the status of its being. Much like a car will indicate when it needs service, our body, too, reacts in the same way. All the tools in this book empower you to become everything your heart desires in this life. It is the desire of the true essence within you to grow and learn. Like any living thing, the more you give what is needed, the more you will grow and thrive rather than just survive, and the better your world will be. You are the driver in your life, so you get to decide where you want to go. Just as you would not leave your house without knowing where you are going, your true nature, your essence in life and "come from" place is what sets into motion every choice you make. You will journey farther and faster when you know your role and align with the core being of yourself. Challenges happen when you do not know your role, or you try to do a role that is not your own. Like actors performing various characters roles over the course of their career, we too wear costumes or personas that may not be how we truly are at the core of our being. Dis-ease and discomfort are side-effects of not being in alignment with your authentic self, as are times when we are feeling challenged by particular people or situations in our life. Like a snake shedding its skin, we are being pushed to grow, to expand. It is at these critical times that it is best to get the lay of the land and update your GPS' mapping system according to the additional information about your journey. When you are really clear about your goals and are in alignment with who you are, your body wisdom will reveal the roadmap to live your best life!

Our body wisdom is the portal into better relationships with yourself and others. It is also the key to getting better results with less effort. If you are ready to stop trying so hard, to reduce the amount of effort you are experiencing in your life but still get the results you are looking for, look no further than your internal mainframe, your body of wisdom system. Following this thread inward allows you to make great progress on your journey while allowing you to live a longer healthier life and produce the results you are after.

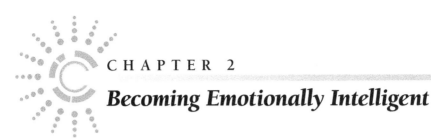

CHAPTER 2
Becoming Emotionally Intelligent

"I've learned that people will forget what you said, people will forget what you did, but people will never forget how you made them feel."
– Carol Buchner

I wanted to travel ever since I was a young girl. My father owned an advertising agency and was well on his way to becoming a millionaire, but he didn't believe in life insurance or financial planning of any kind. His premature death upset any hopes and dreams we had. With my father's income suddenly gone, my mother struggled to care for her two young daughters. Vacations became non-existent, and my world turned upside when my mother moved my sister and me to California, far away from all the friends and family I knew growing up in the suburbs of Chicago. I was excited, however, for the newness of California. Those Golden Gates never shined as brightly as they did on the way to our new home. As a teenager, I longed to be an exchange student so I could travel the world. I applied for the program, got in, and then before I could leave, my mother changed her mind.

As a single mom, I imagine she was terrified of her baby girl traveling halfway around the world to Australia, far beyond her controlling reach. She promised the next year, when I turned sixteen, that I would get to go. As long as I kept up my grades and showed the level of maturity she expected from me, I would have my chance to travel the world. The next year came and

I applied again to the foreign exchange program. I was again admitted and assigned a host family only to have my mother back out a second time. This year she said it was a lack of money. I deduced that she wasn't expecting me to get admitted a second time and since she was a single mom, she likely used that money to take care of my sister and me. Well, that is the way I look at it now.

Back in high school, I had a much different viewpoint, one that accompanied a teenage mind and body overrun by hormones. These stymied attempts to travel were the impetus I needed to break tradition and travel after high school. But how was I going to pay for it? I decided then and there: Instead of attending college, I would join the U.S. Navy. I remember asking the recruiter which rate would get me on board a ship and traveling the world. He replied that women are not allowed on most ships. The ones they were allowed on hardly went anywhere, that is unless I got lucky and earned a coveted spot on a civilian oiler. He said it was rare for that duty to come up and when it did, often went to seasoned sailors who were ready to retire. It was cake duty as far as enlisted personnel were concerned, and I decided I would land that opportunity if it became available. Months went by and I not only became the leader to over fifty women in bootcamp, but I also went on to graduate at the top of my class in A school where I was offered my choice of orders. Two civilian oiler posts came available and I took one of them.

My time in the Navy was a whirlwind of traveling and learning a lot about life and other people, both from areas within my country and those from countries I visited. I was also deeply entrenched in structure, rigidity, and rules. There is no freedom in the military, only chains of command and control. That is what is necessary however, when you are entrusted with protecting and serving the United States Constitution. I learned a lot from my time in the military and was a great sailor; but it all came at a huge cost on my body and I received a medical discharge due to intense and uncontrollable migraines.

After the Navy, I worked in accounting as I pondered what I would do with my career. After a couple of years, I decided it was time to go to college and get my degree so I could start making "real" money. I completed my bachelor's in business administration with a focus in finance. I interned at a large Wall Street firm and decided becoming a financial advisor was the best way to make money and help others to not suffer from the mistakes of my father, whose wealth quickly dissipated upon his death. Back in a male-dominated organization, I again embraced the masculine qualities of structure, competition, and rules. I excelled but again at a cost to my health. It would take many years for me to finally realize that the way I was working was contributing directly to the state of my happiness and wellbeing. Additionally came the crushing blow delivered by my neurologist that accompanied the severity and frequency of migraines: I would never be able to work again. Being placed on permanent disability was a devastating experience for my ego. Who am I if I can't work and make a living on my own? My mother raised my sister and me to be strong, capable women who were not dependent upon a man for our financial future. Her belief became ours and while my sister excelled in her long tenured career, I was failing. It was an incredible wakeup call and what led me down the path of writing this book. Once I learned how to return to a balanced state of being, engaging both my masculine and feminine gifts, I regained my health and now experience the success of getting the results I always wanted in my life. I now get to do work that fulfills me, enjoy the love of a wonderful husband and family, am better able to manage health crises when they arise and continue to travel the world and experience different cultures. If it is possible for me, I know it is possible for you too.

I imagine you are eager to get started, so let us begin by learning more about Lauren. As you've learnt in Chapter 1, Lauren is a client who is struggling to bring out the best in her new team even though she was a top producer in her previous roles. You will follow her journey throughout this book as she learns to identify the areas in her life that are ripe for review and choice, two skills she *thought* she had been utilizing in her life but as she quickly learns not as fully as she really could….

If any these questions resonate and you are willing to learn how to go about righting the ship of your life and charting a smoother course to get to your destination, then this book is for you. Feeling appreciated and engaged in work is the key to retaining good employees according to a new survey by the Society of Human Resource Management. Similarly, research conducted by the US Department of Labor states 64 percent of Americans leave their jobs because they don't feel appreciated and, I would add, understood.

Your efforts to go farther, faster can inhibit the communal needs of individuals in the workplace and detract from the success you can realize. Relationships are a constant in life and your ability to connect with people beyond a surface level provides you a manner in which to get your job done quickly, more easily and with less effort. By applying knowledge learned and applying your own body's innate wisdom, you empower your ability to get things done more effectively than if you use traditional structured methods in business. Additionally, the tools and techniques you learn in *Why Aren't You Listening to Me?* beautifully apply to your personal life as well. Happy and resourceful employees are balanced in both their work and home lives. Millennials entering the work force are quick to remind you that there *is* a better way to build a mousetrap, and the faster you acclimate to a new way of being, the more easily your work and personal life will flow.

As you work your way through this book, keep an open mind and do yourself a favor by giving each technique multiple chances to work for you. As with any new practice or technique, your body and mind must build up muscle memory and experience success while changing the way you relate to others.

CHAPTER 3
Re-Align Your Effort – Make It Worthwhile

"Male and female represent the two sides of the great radical dualism. But in fact, they are perpetually passing into one another. Fluid hardens to solid, solid rushes to fluid. There is no wholly masculine man, no purely feminine woman."
– Margaret Fuller

I have been incredibly curious about people, their beliefs, and why they do the things they do, as well as observing the results they get through their actions. This lifelong love affair with people, cultures, beliefs and personalities has been a path of seeking. I have taken all this knowledge and condensed what I know about people here so that you too could gain from the wisdom of my education and experience. Over the years I have helped many people transform their lives by being mindful of the way they communicate. I advised them on how to make adjustments in the moment by being present, how to create a way of working and being that is in relationship with themselves and others in a way that nourishes their bodies and gets results. It all comes down to one thing: *choice*. If you are anything like my clients, you are living your life doing all the things that *have* to be done, that you *should* do, responding to things that *need* your attention. I would like to invite you to think about your life right now. When is the last time you used these words: *have to, should, need*? I bet it is a large part of your vocabulary whether you are telling someone else they *have to, should, need* to do something, or whether you tell others that *you have to, should, need to* do something. The words we use have a great deal of power and reflect what we value in life. Have you ever thought about the words you use or why you use them? What values are you telling the world you hold?

Exercise: Masculine and Feminine

Within each of us are masculine and feminine qualities. These are the undergarments of the costumes we wear, the way of being we project out into the world. Take a look the list below and place a check mark beside all traits you value in your life:

A	B
Structure	Collaboration
Stability	Community
Directness	Connection
Concise	Intuitive
Providing	Healing
Competition	Loving
Self-Discipline	Nurturing
Hard-working	Open-hearted
Take action	Play
Task-focused	Introspection

If you chose more A's over B's, you are aligned with your masculine qualities. Words from column A are action-oriented, directive in nature, form more structure, are yang, linear, and precise in nature. They are the straight line between A and Z. Words from column B are the pauses in life, the space between the action, yin in nature and where we listen for signals and information which guides our way. There is nothing inherently wrong with either column, but rather a launching point in which we can begin.

Lauren discovered she valued many of the facets in column A, and that many facets in column B made her feel uncomfortable and are a bit "out there." When I asked which ones in particular she struggled with, she told me intuitive, healing, nurturing, lean back, and play. I knew immediately this was where she could begin the process of understanding where she is right now as well as give her a starting point in which to examine how she is living her life. I explained to Lauren how we all have innate gifts within us and when we accept these gifts we utilize the qualities and achieve greater results with a lot less effort. She was curious how this could be done, so I shared with her about the gifts I noticed in her.

"Lauren, I bet you are strong, resilient, and overcome just about all challenges put in front of you. I bet you get great results when you are in control of a task, and I bet the task gets done professionally and directly."

She stifles a smile just enough for the corners of her lips to curl upward. She looks amused.

"I also bet that the reason you are not getting the results you used to get is because you have a lot more people on your team that are much different than you. I bet too, that you are frustrated that you are the one being asked to change the way you communicate. Tell me what that is like for you?"

The look in Lauren's eyes intensifies as she details the story of her boss asking her to change despite her getting exceptional results. I interrupt and ask her again, "Tell me what being told to change your style of communication is like for you to hear from your boss?"

She stares at me for a few moments, looking like she is deciding whether to attack what I just said.

"Why do I always have to be the one to change? Why is it I am not okay the way I am?" Tears fill her eyes.

I inquire, "What is in your tears?".

"Stress. Exhaustion. Pain".

"What's it like to feel so much stress, exhaustion and pain?"

"It's tiring. I just want to get things done but it seems I am being blocked every time I turn around ever since I took this promotion. I don't know what happened to stop me from getting the results I used to get!"

Has this ever happened to you? You are cruising along with a plan, and then *wham*! Something happens and you begin to question if you took a wrong turn somewhere. Truth is, every step you took was a choice made by you. Before you balk at what I just said, hear me out. Every step is a choice made by you either consciously or unconsciously. The latter is where we will focus for now, as these are the beliefs and perspectives that are formed throughout our lives to help us understand and interact with the world around us. It is basically our lizard brain (the amygdala) that doesn't speak spoken or written language. It is highly skilled at doing just one thing, keeping your body alive. When this part of your brain makes decisions, it is doing so from past experience. When you were a little child, you were told beliefs and perspectives that your parents or caretakers had. Some of it was very useful, "Don't touch the hot stove or your hand will get burned," "Look both ways before you cross the street or else you could get hit by a car," but much of it was just regurgitation of the beliefs and perspectives that were fed to your parents by their parents and caretakers. Quite frankly, many of us have beliefs and perspectives in place that we do not even agree with right now. But like a song playing in the background, you tune out the noise and forget it is playing. Examining these beliefs and perspectives is taking account of the automatic systems you have in place which are the foundation of your professional and personal relationships.

"I am curious, tell me more about the people you are having challenges with at work."

Her body shifts uncomfortably in her maroon velour tufted chair.

"Well, there is no one office or person in particular, but the people I seem to have the most issue getting on board with my direction just aren't listening to me. They have solid books of business, their numbers are not bad; but every time I meet with them or read their emails, they keep going on and on about everything. I want them to get straight to the point, and not mince words. When I tell them to do that, they seem shocked and hurt. They are so sensitive! What is worse, is they end up doing the bare minimum and the bare minimum just isn't going to cut it for me in making my sales goals."

I nod my head slowly and ask, "What is it like for you to deal with sensitive people?"

"Ugh, kill me now! I am so over sensitive people. I hate feeling like I have to walk on eggshells every time I encounter one of them. They just need to grow a set, you know? Join the real world and spend more time working and less time chatting." She rolls her eyes to accentuate her displeasure.

"Would you like to play a game with me?"

Lauren stiffens up, her lip curls slightly as she draws her chin slowly back and away from me. She is distrusting of what I just said. I wonder if it is because she has forgotten how to play or is it because she sees no value in it?

"What about what I just said do you distrust?"

Lauren's eyes open wide and she says, "It just makes me uncomfortable. Aren't you here to help me get my advisor's on board with my plan? How is playing a game going to help?"

"You never know unless you try, right? If playing doesn't help us get anywhere, then I promise we can try another approach, okay?"

Lauren nods her head in agreement, and we proceed.

"The topic we are going to play with is "sensitive people." Your current perspective on sensitive people is that you feel like you have to walk on eggshells with them, that they spend too much time chatting and not enough time working, they just need to grow a set of balls, kill me now already, correct?"

Lauren smirks and answers yes.

"What do you notice in your body when you think these thoughts?"

"I don't know. Nothing."

"If you were to imagine that you felt something in your body, where would you feel it?"

Lauren ponders my words and then touches her hand to her belly, "I guess I feel it right here."

I place my hand on my belly in the same location as Lauren and ask, "What do you feel right here?"

She begins, "I feel tightness, some burning. I guess what I ate for lunch isn't fully agreeing with me," she smirks.

"What about sensitive people doesn't agree with you?" I ask.

"They get me fired up! I just want to get shit done and they are so slow and want to talk so much!".

"What else are you noticing in your body when you think about sensitive people?"

"I am noticing my neck muscles are getting tighter and my head is beginning to pound. I think I need to take some aspirin."

"Okay," I say, "what one-word or short phrase would you use to describe what you are feeling now?"

Lauren winces as she feels into herself, "'Pain in the ass' is what I am thinking."

"Okay, 'pain in the ass' is what we will call this perspective."

"Perspective?" Lauren asks.

"Yes, what you feel about sensitive people is the perspective you hold, the lens in which you use to view anyone you deem as sensitive. Much like putting on a pair of glasses, we all use varying lenses to view, understand and maneuver in our world. Your current perspective is 'pain in the ass,' so now I'd like you to stand up and imagine this perspective is a very wet coat. Shake your body and imagine this coat falling heavily and easily to the floor. Then take one step to your left." Lauren follows my direction and we continue, "Now, thinking about sensitive people, I'd like you to tell me the first animal that comes to mind?"

"Sheep," she says.

"Okay, tell me about sheep?"

"Well, they are small, white, fluffy and they don't really go anywhere unless a Shepard guides them."

"What else about sheep comes to mind?"

"They like to hang out together, I always see them moving in herds."

"What do you know about sheep?"

"They eat grass, and don't do much else I guess."

"Interesting. Your sheep sound a lot like how you feel about your advisors."

We both smile, then I ask, "What do you think makes a sheep happiest?"

"I guess eating grass and hanging out with other sheep."

"How do you feel when you hang out with your friends over a meal?"

"Pretty good I guess, it's fun."

"Pretty good, fun. Hmmm... When was the last time you hung out with your friends over a meal?"

"Hah! It's been a long time! I've been pretty busy with work and the family lately."

"Okay" I said, "Remember the last time you had a meal with a really good friend. What was it like for you?"

Lauren smiles genuinely and her eyes look off into the distance.

"It felt so good! Seriously, my work was going great, I was making a lot of money and I was having fun with Becca my best friend from college. We had an amazing meal, great wine and laughed so hard Becca nearly peed her pants! I felt like I didn't have a care in the world."

She laughs at the memory and I smile, "What if sensitive people were like these sheep, spending their lives enjoying delicious grass and hanging out with their best friends and family all the time? What would you imagine that would be like? Not having a care in the world?"

"It sounds like a pretty awesome way to live! I am actually getting a little jealous of these sheep!"

She laughs again and I notice her shoulders have visibly dropped and the lines on her face have softened.

"What one-word or short phrase would you like to call this perspective?"

"Not a care in the world."

I smile and then invite her to imagine the wet coat again and instruct her to shake it off.

"I'd like you to take a giant step forward now and tell me, what is the first thing you see?"

Lauren does as I ask, and she replies, "I see a picture of my husband and me with our kids on the beach in Maui. I won president's club that year. It was a great trip!"

"What made that trip so great?"

"Well for one, I had a lot of time with my kids, watching them play with their dad in the sand and having their laughter fill the air. The weather was perfect, and we were treated to some really amazing food."

"Sounds wonderful! What else are you noticing as you remember this vacation?"

"I remember how relaxed I felt, I wasn't suffering from back or head pain. I just felt really good."

"Great! I'd like you to tell me what you are feeling in your body right now?" Lauren closes her eyes and replies, "I feel happy and warm."

"Where are you feeling the 'happy and warm' feelings?" She smiles and places both her hands over her heart. I place my hands over my heart too and ask, "With these warm and happy thoughts I'd like you to think about sensitive people. What are you noticing now?"

Lauren drops lower into her body and shifts her weight to one leg.

"I am noticing that sensitive people I know are pretty chill and laid back. It is actually kind of a nice way of seeing them, like I am seeing them for who they really are in this moment."

"And what is it like for you to see sensitive people this way?"

"Well, I think they know something I don't, and I'd like to figure out what that is!" I nod my head in agreement.

"I'd like you to once again give me a word or short phrase to represent this point of view."

"Relaxed and happy."

"Great. Imagine that wet coat again, shaking your body and allowing it to fall completely to the floor. I'd like you to take a big step right and turn around 180 degrees."

Lauren does as I ask again and then I say, "Looking at the topic 'sensitive people', I'd like us to review the perspectives we have played with and then I would like to invite you to choose the perspective that resonates with you." Lauren nods her head in agreement.

"Which perspective feels the best when you think of 'sensitive people'? Pain in the ass?"

"No," she replies quickly.

"How about not a care in the world?"

"That one seems pretty good, but seems like a lofty, aimless way of being." "Okay, how about relaxed and happy?"

"Yes, that one feels the best! I could really see the sensitive people in my life in a new light with that perspective. I can see how having fun and enjoying what they are doing can feel relaxing and enjoyable."

"Wonderful that you can see the gifts that sensitive people you know offer you. With that knowledge in mind, what would best help you to cement what you have learned here today?"

Lauren pauses and replies, "I think this picture worked great at reminding me of that feeling and I think it would help if I remembered it."

"Great! Your homework for next week is to load this picture on your phone, then set a reminder to go off every hour. When the timer goes off, set a timer for five minutes and I want you to look at the picture on your phone and remember these feelings you experienced just now."

Lauren rolls her brown eyes and says, "That is impossible! I can't do that!"

"You have a choice Lauren, you can say yes, no or give me a counteroffer of what you can do."

"Well, I can put a reminder in my phone for once each day and then look at the picture for five minutes."

I challenge her to do it three times a day, or every time she sits down for a meal and she agrees.

"One last question before I leave, what are you experiencing in your body right now?"

Lauren pauses and closes her eyes, "I feel good, relaxed and happy."

"Do you still need that aspirin?" I ask.

"No," she laughs and smiles a gorgeous grin.

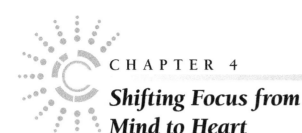

CHAPTER 4
Shifting Focus from Mind to Heart

"The intuitive mind is a sacred gift and the rational mind is a faithful servant. We have created a society that honors the servant and has forgotten the gift."
– Albert Einstein

The next time I spoke with Lauren, I checked in with her about how her homework went. She reported that she really enjoyed the exercise and that she was feeling slightly more relaxed than when we first spoke.

"What would you like to receive some coaching on today?" I ask.

"Although the homework exercise was good, I am still struggling with getting people to do what I tell them to do. I have so much work that needs to get done and I am still not feeling great between these headaches and my back hurting."

"What is it like to be in pain and have so much on your plate?" I inquire.

"It sucks but I guess it is how it has to be if you want to get things done. No pain, no gain, right?"

"Who told you this is how it has to be?"

Lauren thinks about that for a moment and replies, "My father, I guess. He worked really hard, long days, and I recall him looking exhausted and in pain most nights he came home. My mom would make him a drink and he would watch television a bit after dinner while my mom and I cleaned up. He always provided for us and didn't really complain about how much pain he was in, but my mom would often remind me not to push him too much and I could always tell he was uncomfortable. I guess I figured that to be successful you need to do whatever it takes whether you are in pain or working long hours. My dad used to tell me, 'Suck it up buttercup' whenever I complained that my homework was too long or if I wasn't feeling well. He told me I didn't know what real pain was, but now I do."

"Where do you notice the belief of 'suck it up buttercup' appearing in your life right now?"

Lauren thinks for a few moments, "A lot of places. Certainly in my work, but also in the way I raise my children and even with my husband. It is what causes many of our fights, my husband just doesn't get how much effort I put into everything getting results, or the toll it is taking on my body."

"Tell me about the effort you make to get results?"

Lauren sighs and slumps a bit in her chair. "I work so many hours and make all the money for our family. My husband and I decided that he would be the one to stay home with the children since I have always done so well financially. Besides, he is great with children and they laugh and play for hours together. I wish I could be like that, but I just can't."

"Who told you you can't laugh and play?" I ask her.

She pauses again for a long time and then replies, "I don't know. I guess I am just not the playful, laughing type."

Do you relate to Lauren and find yourself working hard in order to get things done without having much time for fun, laughter, and play? If you hold the belief that you have to work hard to get where you want to go, I would ask, "How is that working in all areas of your life?" Many of my clients who are driven and result-orientated are exceptional workers. Whether they are entrepreneurs, C-suite, managers or employees, their common denominator is that they desire to get things done, but their bodies and personal lives pay the price for working so hard and with so much effort. Their personal relationships are often either nonexistent or strained. These clients are achievers, focused and rigidly defined by structure in their life. Often times they are accused of being control freaks. Does this sound like anyone you know? Have you been accused of being this way? Structure is great and necessary in our lives. After all, we need boundaries to be able to freely express ourselves and live a joyful life. However, too much structure, too rigid beliefs and inflexibility end up draining our bodies and making us sick. Women in particular are vulnerable to a host of health conditions if their life is too controlled and they are not fully in touch with their emotions and feelings. These women often deny their feelings or have beliefs that they are not worthy which could not be farther from the truth. Marianne Williamson says in *A Return to Love*, "Our deepest fear is not that we are inadequate. Our deepest fear is that we are powerful beyond measure. It is our light, not our darkness that most frightens us. We ask ourselves, 'Who am I to be brilliant, gorgeous, talented, fabulous?' Actually, who are you not to be? You are a child of God. Your playing small does not serve the world. There is nothing enlightened about shrinking so that other people won't feel insecure around you. We are all meant to shine, as children do. We were born to make manifest the glory of God that is within us. It's not just in some of us; it's in everyone. And as we let our own light shine, we unconsciously give other people permission to do the same. As we are liberated from our own fear, our presence automatically liberates others." I would like to explore what is going on in your life with you and I ask that you remain open to the tools I teach you in this book. Everyone has feelings and whether you are in touch with them or not determines your overall mental and physical wellbeing and the state of relationship you have with yourself. Of course, I am referring to the majority of people on the bell curve here, not the extremists – narcissists, sociopaths, etc. Rather ordinary people like you, me, and my clients.

When we don a personality type that is not in alignment with our authentic selves, I refer to it as wearing a costume. Much like the clothes that actors wear, our costumes are the traits of leader, spokesperson, researcher, and collaborator. A costume I have worn a lot in my life is that of a leader. Although I am at times called to bring forth that aspect of myself it is not my preferred state of being, but rather the costume I wear because I believe it is needed at times to be successful and fulfilled. Not knowing any better, I learned this way of being by watching how my mother interacted with the world. Knowing this about myself has enabled me to be more productive with a lot less effort. Would you like to know how? You are in the right place, as the upcoming chapters will guide you through the system I use myself and what I have taught many others as well. I call it the Conscious Heart Awareness Technique (CHAT) and it works with everyone who has an open mind and willingness to allow it to take root in your life. In the coming chapters, I teach you techniques and practices that you can use to realize better results, improve your ability to communicate with anyone and do all of this with a lot less effort than you are exerting right now. Along the way, you are likely to learn that you are able to trust yourself and others too, which naturally elevates your ability to produce lasting results. Don't worry, I won't be telling you that you need to change your religious beliefs or join a cult in order to make this happen. In fact, my techniques and practices will empower you so that you can live the life *you* choose, whatever that may be. There are some guidelines along the way that I ask you to follow, but they are basic governances that exist in order to grant you the most freedom to live your life fully. Once again, you have the choice to accept them or not. This is your one fabulous, juicy, wondrous life, so choose wisely. In the upcoming chapters, you will learn the Conscious Heart Awareness Technique as well as all the benefits, tools and practices you need to apply this method to your life right now.

CHAPTER 5

Effective Communication – The Key to Relationship Success

"Progress is impossible without change, and those who cannot change their minds cannot change anything."
– George Bernard Shaw

As multiple personality indicator tests have shown, people display attributes of typical archetypes. Not everyone is purely one archetype, but rather are a mix of many types with one defining archetype which desires to come forward. This is who you are at the very center of your being, and at times is also the costume you wear in life. More importantly, it is a place to begin examining what gifts are available to you. People are complex. Just as you can learn to speak any foreign language but become stymied by varying accents in a given country, learning the nuances of archetype traits are meant to be a basis for exploration rather than a hard and fast rule. The four types below are representative of many personality systems in existence. Each one examines who you are in your most conscious state as well as who you are in your most unconscious state.

There are four types of personality archetypes identified below: Leader, Spokesperson, Researcher and Collaborator. There are more that can be named, but these are the main types that you will recognize being expressed in people around you. Who are you at the core of your being? How do you relate to the world around you?

Personality Archetypes

Leader

These are the take-charge people, eager to make decisions and give direction. They are often single focused getting results and likely have experienced success getting there. These are the action takers in our world. They are focused on execution and the results produced. They are not interested in discussions to discover answers, but rather consult a trusted advisor, mentor or confidant to gain insight on a situation. When you communicate with a Leader, speak with authority and confidence in your voice, directing them to what needs to be done. Stand tall, chin held high, and shoulders back. If you are confident in your manner, it is likely they will not waste time taking action.

In their most conscious form, Leaders are confident, secure and lead with compassion and understanding. They are relaxed and are able to see the meta view as well as any challenges that could arise while striving for their goal. The unconscious aspects of this archetype can be a perfectionist, critical, insecure and lead from a place of fear and vulnerability. They do not have a well thought-out plan and make decisions that cost them their goals because they take action from a mindset of fear. They really want to get through all the tasks in their day but their uncertainty about how they will get it done often stymies their progress because their fear leads them to making poor choices and cost them valuable time and effort.

The best way to connect with a Leader is to ask them how you can help and be willing to do what they say in the manner in which they tell you to do it. They would much prefer to do things themselves because they like things done a particular way but will be more likely to welcome your assistance if they can count on you to follow their direction. Make sure you are able to do the task a Leader requests without complaining and with a positive attitude. These individuals are on a time schedule and don't have the bandwidth to deal with grumpy, sad, or other time-consuming emotions. They appreciate solutions so give them a solid answer to their problem and let them be on their way.

Spokesperson

These are the visionaries with big ideas but who may not be very good at the minutia involved to make them a reality. These are the risk takers, the early adopters. They appreciate being praised for their efforts and want to be seen for the forward-thinking ideas and out of the box solutions they create. If they do not think something is fun, they are likely to procrastinate getting the task done. When you communicate with a Spokesperson, speak with confidence and strength in your voice. Be lighthearted in your request and intonation in your voice. Direct them to what needs to be done and let them come up with the way in which they do it.

In their most conscious form, Spokespersons are gregarious, fun-loving, and desire to make a positive impact on the world around them. They are excellent at bringing fun to situations so give them some room to bring their own unique style to what needs to happen. You will be surprised by the creative thinking that comes from this personality type. The unconscious aspects of this archetype are rebellious and more likely to operate outside of the legal or moral ways of doing business. They can struggle with staying in the confines of structure and can be at a higher risk of breaking rules.

The best way to connect with a Spokesperson is to tell them how much you appreciate their contributions to the goal. Be specific and point out their positive character or personality traits when you compliment them. They love receiving accolades for their effort and what they contribute to the team, so feel free to do so one on one or in front of others if you would like to garner more of their support in the future.

Researcher

These are the thinkers, the people who take the big ideas of the Spokesperson and develop a systematic approach to executing them. They are interested in the minutia; their decisions are well thought out and they ask lots of questions. They want to be valued and admired for their input on how to achieve the desired goal. When communicating with a Researcher, speak with a softer tone in your voice and ask them what solutions they have that could help to accomplish the task and be patient while they ask lots of follow up questions.

In their most conscious form, Researchers are calm, centered and secure they can do what you request. They want to really understand the issue so that they can create a system to make it easier for others. They are slow and steady, reliable and patient. The unconscious aspects of this archetype can be intelligent but insecure which can lead to being distrustful. They keep to themselves and because they are more often introverted in nature, can focus their frustrations inward and be moody, melancholy and hold a grudge.

The best way to connect with a Researcher is to tell them how much you admire and appreciate their contributions to the team. Tell them you value their education and experience and reward them with experiences they would enjoy for a job well done. Whether you buy them dinner, give them tickets to a sporting or music event, or even invite them to attend a conference in a highly regarded location, the way you show your admiration and gratitude will convey your willingness to connect with these dedicated individuals.

Collaborator

These are the team builders and relationship makers. They are the ones who make sure everyone works together to get the idea to market. They will move mountains if you ask them to do things and make them feel included in the process. They have a deep desire to get to know the people involved, how it will impact them and how they can make any transitions easier. When communicating with a Collaborator, speak with kindness, softer tone, and give them space to feel comfortable. Allow time to connect and involve them in the plan. They work best when they feel they are included and when you appreciate the gifts they have to offer to the goal.

In their most conscious form, they are the nurturers and are focused upon lifting others up and including them. They are happy, easy going and want people to feel comfortable and all work together to make things happen. The unconscious aspect of this archetype is highly skilled at manipulating emotions, but they do it for attention rather than ill intent. Moodiness and emotional outbursts are more likely because they can be insecure and fear-based in their thinking, feeling like a victim of their circumstances.

The best way to connect with a Collaborator is to really get to know who they are and what ways they like to help. They want you to listen and hear what is happening for them. Resist your urge to come up with a quick solution and leave. Their driving need is to be of service, and they will feel valued and honored by your personal attention. Keep in mind that they may not want to spend too much time around people that have intense natures as it can disrupt the calm and harmonious environment they prefer to create.

Lauren's biggest struggle is with Collaborators in her district, though she has revealed that she is having trouble reaching the Researchers as well. She does a fair enough job with the Spokesperson types, however even they are doing the bare minimum because Lauren is not allowing them the freedom to be creative in the execution with their clients. Because Lauren is so fixed on how people get what she wants done, she ignores the needs of her individual advisors and managers while giving the impression that she simply does not care about them or the contributions they make to district goals.

Now that you know more about personality types, I would like you to think about the following questions: Do you trust yourself? Do you take risks in your life and make mistakes? Or do you prefer instead to take little risk and stay within the comforting lines of structure? Whether you are a willing risk-taker and mistake-maker or a restrained risk-taker and gain comfort from structure, tells me a lot about how you approach life. In the book *Mindset: The New Psychology of Success* Stanford University Psychologist Carol S. Dweck describes what fixed and growth mindsets are and helps you to identify what type of mindset you possess. Knowing your own mindset type and how it influences your approach to work, empowers you to examine your life with keener understanding and appreciation. People with a growth mindset are more likely to believe that your basic qualities are things that can be changed, can be cultivated through your efforts. Once again, there is no judgment about what type of mindset you possess. Everything is knowledge and knowledge is power. The more aware you become, the easier your life will flow. You feel empowered to make choices that are aligned with your values and you will experience better results with less effort.

Exercise

Values

I would like you to think about what your values are in life. Write a list of values you recognize in yourself. Take some time with this and when you are done, look back over the list and pick out the top five that really resonate with you. Start by making a list of all the values you recognize in yourself, then write the top five down to use for a later exercise.

Life Map

Everyone can use a map when they are in uncharted territory. The life map below will help you determine where you are in your life. I have included another copy in the Appendix at the back of the book that you can copy and use for future check ins with yourself. For now, I would like you to rank your satisfaction in the following areas of your life from one to ten with ten being the most fulfilled and one being the least fulfilled.

Today's Date:

Career:	Family:	Health:
Fun:	Friendships:	Money:
Significant Other:	Personal Growth:	

CHAPTER 6

Conscious Heart Awareness Technique

"Effective communication is 20 percent what you know and 80 percent how you feel about what you know."
– Jim Rohn

The Conscious Heart Awareness Technique (CHAT) was developed to help my clients learn the skills of presence as well as provide a map to the innate gifts you have buried deep within yourself. At the centermost core of your being is your true, authentic self. Your personality and mindset are tools that help know yourself better by giving you clues to beliefs that are operating in your body system. The work you are doing right now, the relationships you have, and the way you live are threads strewn with beliefs and perspectives leading to your innermost being. Your lives and experiences are all unique unto yourself. None of us are exactly the same. We each have varying filters in which we see and experience life. It is the awareness that you *have* filters that empowers you further. Turning inward and slowing down your pace in life is what helps you to read the signs that guide your way. If you are driving 100 miles an hour, you are far less likely to catch any but the largest signs along the road. The slower you go, the smaller the signs can be and still allow you to read them. These signposts give you valuable information about your journey like, "Cliff ahead" or "Curves for the next thirty miles" as well as the direction in which you are traveling. When you are not in full relationship with yourself at this level, you experience unnecessary challenges, communication breakdowns, exhaustion, heart break, confusion, and dis-ease. When you follow these threads back to the source of your innermost being, you are empowered to make choices that are in alignment with who you are at a base level and thereby reveal to you the map of your life.

Each of us is empowered to choose our own journey through life. Where you are born becomes your starting point in the world and each decision you make – from the most grandiose "I am marrying the love of my life" to the smallest, simplest decision "read this book now" – creates the path you journey in your body during this one and only time. I will never again be Teresa Lodato when my body dies, but the innermost part of me will continue to exist. It is the air in every one of my cells, it is life force, spirit, God, Goddess, energy, source. No matter the name you use, each person with even an ounce of this essence in their body breathes air. Fear cannot breathe air unless it latches on to an unsuspecting, unaware human. The weaker the essence of life is within you, the more susceptible you are to making decisions based in fear. The stronger the essence of life is within you, the more you utilize *all* the signs along your journey, even the ones that read "delicious food next exit" or "meeting Mr. Right next left."

CHAT involves three parts: first, becoming conscious, aware of what is going on within you right here in this moment. Second, you follow the thread of sensations (pain or pleasure are most powerful to motivate you, but there are many portals to getting in deeper connection with yourself), as well as your beliefs and perspectives that lead you to release any barrier that keeps you from knowing and being the truth of who you are: powerful, strong, connected. The system you have programmed within yourself is your version of auto pilot in your life. Much like a computer program establishes rules and code (if this, then that), your beliefs and perspectives are automatic. Lastly, you bring this awareness back to the surface of your life so you can engage in relationship with those around you in a way that is truly authentic and true to yourself from your deepest core to your outermost being. This is the eye of the storm, the centering, the place of greatest clarity and empowerment.

Lauren arrives at my office looking exhausted and frazzled. She plops down on my brown leather wingback chair and slumps over, nearly on the verge of tears.

"I almost never cry" she exclaims. "This day has just been horrible though. What is worse, it has been a horrible week, too."

I sit and listen, "Tell me, what you would like some coaching on today?" I watch as she tries to compose herself. I sit silently watching her and waiting. Several minutes go by and then she begins, "My district is in third to last place in the nation. *The nation*!" she exclaims. "Never in my life have I been so low. Never in my life have I sunk to such levels."

"What is it like for you to not to be the top producer any longer?"

My question goes right to the core of her pain and she steels herself against it, absorbing the words as if she is pushing a sword more deeply into her body to prove she could handle it.

"It's embarrassing. I was always an A student, always graduated at the top of my class. I am humiliated."

"What is going on in your body right now?"

She replies, "My head is throbbing, my lower back is tight and achy, my stomach hurts."

"What is present for you now in these feelings of humiliation?"

"I am feeling frustrated, hurt and like I am not getting the support I need at work or at home. My easy-going husband is even more distant, and I fear he no longer loves me. I have really been riding him hard lately and I can't help but feel like he might end up leaving me. Money is tight since I am on a salary these days without my bonuses, even though I get paid a lot of money, it is not the same as the commissions I once made as an advisor or managing advisor. I feel like I want to cry."

"What's stopping you from crying right now?"

"I don't know." I watch as tears well up in her eyes and threaten to overflow onto her high cheekbones.

"What is present for you in this moment?" I ask.

"I just don't know how much more I can take. I have to be so tough and strong out there and I just can't take it anymore." She breaks down in tears as I sit holding space for those precious frozen emotions she has bottled up over the years that succumb to the heat in this moment and begin to flow.

Lauren is very near or perhaps even at her rock bottom. When this happens, there is a release, a surrendering to what is present in your life. Often times you are unwilling to see how your behaviors, beliefs, perspectives are affecting your life, let alone change them. That is where I am able to help. It is vital to know where you are before you can chart a course of action to where you want to be. When you are completely unaware of your blind spots that hold you back from living a life worthy of yourself, you are moving at such a fast pace that you scarcely have time to pause and reflect upon what you are missing. Other times you can be so focused on the end result that your blinders prevent you from seeing the signs along the way that caution you are getting off track. What are you doing right now to make sure what happened to Lauren does not happen for you?

There are a few questions I would like you to consider. The first one: Is it more important for you to be *right* or be in *relationship*? This can be a tough one for many of my clients as they are so accustomed to getting their own way that they think they *shouldn't have to* choose. The fact is, whether you choose either perspective or demand both perspectives, it really does not matter to the other person. The other person is going to feel what you are saying just by the words you choose, so choose wisely. If you demand to have it both ways, what you are really saying to the other person is "I don't care what you think, I don't care what you want. All that matters is me and what I want and need." Sounds pretty selfish, doesn't it? The sad fact is that when people view life from this perspective, they end up being the ones who are miserable because they remove themselves from experiencing emotionally intimate relationships where they can get clues to themselves and their journey. The better you are at noticing the signs within yourself, the more gifts you uncover to live your best life!

The next thing I would like you to consider is the manner in which you speak your words as well as your body language. As any actor will tell you, intonation and body language are the foundation to conveying your emotion and state of being in a crystal-clear manner. Since your words convey so much, it is vital that you speak and present your language from an authentic way of being. It is important that the words spoken come from the heart. Have you ever listened to someone who is passionate about what they are saying? Their words have power to move you, to compel you into taking action and they can easily do so without yelling or hurting themselves or others while they speak. Their words are filled with the emotion they are experiencing. Whether it comes from a place of love or fear, is evident in their choice of words, how they speak them as well as their emotional state at the time being. This may seem like a common concept, but I invite you to stop and think about the people in your life. Do each and every one of the people in your life understand *and* put this in practice? Given the state of the world right now, I say unequivocally no. The challenge in your modern world is to grow, to evolve, to change. If there is life, there is growth. If you are not growing and changing, then you are dying. It is your choice; you get to decide what you want to do with this one precious life you are living right now.

Exercise

Presence

Eckhart Tolle wrote *The Power of Now.* If you haven't read it, I wholeheartedly recommend you doing so. I recall my first read through of it over ten years ago and the epiphanies I experienced were life-changing. It was like someone had peeled away layer after layer of my being and exposed me fully to the truth that is. Presence is the power of now.

For this exercise I invite you to place your attention in your hands. What does this book feel like in your hands right now? What does the cover feel like? The pages? If you are reading on an electronic device, what does it feel like? Is it cool? Hot? Smooth? Being in touch with our bodies allows us to experience our world and directly interact with it.

You are a co-creator of your life so the more present you become, the better you are able to make choices that align with your inner being, your authentic self. When you tune into the core of who you are, you are empowered to live your unique life and in that space, there is no comparison, no competition. Just as a mustard seed can never grow into an oak tree, you too can never become anyone other than yourself. When you realize this, really take a moment to let that sink in, you release the need to manipulate and control another or to dim your light, and instead become what you are meant to be. Each life is a snowflake, you are unique unto yourself and it is your birth right to live your life fully and to experience everything you can. I often think of our bodies as avatars. It is your innermost being that moves the avatar. Like a video game where you manipulate avatars through differing scenarios, challenges and storylines, your innermost being directs your life through the daily challenges, moment to moment making adjustments that chart your course along the journey of your life. As avatars become more advanced through virtual reality, you can experience more fully what it is like to be the being who drives the action. In that awareness is where you find the opportunity to be fully present in your own life.

"What is present for you now?" I ask Lauren after her tears have subsided.

Her shoulders droop downward, and head is heavy in her hands. She looks up with tear-stained cheeks, black lines of mascara streaking down her face.

"Emptiness."

"What is present in the emptiness?" Lauren inhales deeply and slowly.

"I feel like I have no place left to go. I am at the bottom of deep dark pit."

"What are you noticing from this deep, dark place?"

"I am noticing that there is only me."

"What does it feel like in this deep, dark place?"

"Surprisingly, like nothing. It is neither hot nor cold. It just is."

"How does it feel to be in this deep, dark place?"

"Safe. I am held. I feel supported by something as if I am firmly on the ground."

"The ground floor. The elevator only goes up from here," I say to her.

She forces a smile then takes another deep breath in and out.

"What else is here for you right now?" Lauren pauses and takes another deep breath.

"I am noticing there is no clutter. I am clear."

"What is in your clarity?"

"I feel like I can breathe again. I feel like I can think clearly again, like the fog has lifted."

"From this place of clarity, what is possible for you now?"

"I have the urge to stand up and dust myself off."

"Well, then let us stand up and dust ourselves off!" We smile at one another, stand up and use our hands to figuratively dust ourselves off.

"What is here right now?" I ask.

"I am noticing that even though I have gone through a lot, I am still here. My ego may be bruised, but I am still here."

"Right here, right now?" I say to her.

"Right here, right now," Lauren replies back to me.

Exercise: Awareness Technique

When you are deeply rooted in the present moment, you are providing a structure in which to hold yourself firmly while you expand and contract. Oxygen moves through your body in the same way, with your lungs expanding and contracting, propelling this vital source of life through your entire system. When your feet become roots firmly grounded in the earth, you too are grounded in the beliefs and perspectives that shape your thoughts and make your choices. Like a hurricane that swirls and thrusts whatever is in its path of destruction, your thoughts can swirl and thrust you into action unconsciously if you are not aware. Grounding helps you to move out of the fierce winds into the calming center in the eye of the storm. In this exercise, you will be rooting yourself deeply to the present moment by bringing your awareness into your body. This exercise is best done in a sitting position, but once you get the hang of it you can do it standing up or even lying down. Read through this exercise first so you become aware of what you will be doing. If you have a busy overthinking mind, give it a bone to gnaw on and keep it occupied for a while, for what we are about to do generally helps satiate its hyperaware state.

Place both feet firmly on the ground. Roll your neck and shoulders slowly in circles one way a few times, then the opposite direction a few times. Take a deep inhalation into your belly (diaphragm) slowly in through your nose to the count of five, then pause before exhaling slowly to the count of seven through your mouth. While at rest most people take about ten to fourteen breaths per minute. With this exercise you want to reduce the breaths to about seven to ten per minute. Do not get too stressed by this, however, just breathe deeply and slowly as best you can. With practice you will get better at it. Close your eyes. Doing so removes unnecessary distractions so you can bring your full attention to what is present for you right here, right now. Bring your attention to your feet. Become aware of what it feels like to have your feet resting firmly on the floor. What are you feeling? Maybe it is the insoles of your shoes, or the texture of the ground or floor if you are barefoot. Whatever you are noticing just allow it to be. Without judgment, without forcing anything to happen. Bring your attention to the top of your head. Imagine you are standing beneath a shower of silvery blue water falling gently upon the top of your head. Imagine this water has the ability to flow easily through your body starting at the crown of your head. Its flow is the light that you will follow as you move your awareness throughout your body. If you would like, you can place your hands on the top of your head to help bring your awareness to this area. As you do this, feel free to massage your scalp, stroke your hair or just gently rest your hands upon your head. Do whatever you feel is appropriate for your head and just give it your full attention. Observe what you are noticing, then let these thoughts go.

As the silvery blue water flows down into your head, bring your awareness to the area right behind your eyes. You can place your hands over your eyes if you would like and then just breathe in and out slowly a few times. Move your fingertips over to your temples now and gently massage them in little circles, first one way then the other. Move your hands to the back of your head, to the bony structure at the base of your skull, the occipital ridge. Slowly circle your fingertips along the tendons along the ridge, releasing any tension held there. What are you noticing in this area? Observe what comes up for you and then let everything go. As the warm silver blue rain falls gently through your head, allow your hands to follow the water down into your neck. Place one or both hands on your neck, bringing your awareness there. Give your neck a rub with your hands or fingertips, allowing them to massage the sides and back of your neck. What are you noticing? Observe it and let it go. As the water flows down into your shoulders and chest, allow your hands to follow the water, gently massaging or touching your body as you bring your awareness fully into the present moment. As you do so, you are consciously affirming to your body your gratitude and desire to be in relationship with it fully. Take one hand and reach across your chest to the opposite shoulder and release the other arm down to your side. Massage or touch the area between your neck and shoulders. Bring your awareness there. Observe what comes up for you and let the thoughts go.

Bring your awareness now into your chest and upper back. Here allow some of the silvery blue water to flow also down into each arm and into all your fingertips. Use your hands to massage your chest and each arm. What comes up for you? Observe without judging. You are doing just fine. Release all the thoughts that come up for you. Like a balloon, imagine you release the string and allow the balloon to float up and away into the sky. Let it go.

Slowly move your awareness to your middle back and stomach just behind your belly button. Move your hands to this area and give your body some attention and love by resting your hands there or massaging it. Continue to notice what comes up for you and then just let it go, continue breathing deeply and slowly.

Now move your awareness slowly into your hips and your

lower back. Allow your hands to rest, or gently massage your hips and low back. Observe what comes up for you and let it go.

As the beautiful water flows effortlessly down each leg, follow with your attention. Bring your hands to each leg and touch or massage each one, down through the tops of your legs, through your knees and into your calves, ankles, and lastly your feet. All this happens with no effort, just as water flows over your skin. Imagine the feeling of your feet and legs becoming rooted into the floor and earth below you. If you have trouble imagining this, then just pretend. Take notice of any sensations you feel but again, do not judge them. Soft attention is the best practice. As the roots of the tree reach further and further away from your body and deep into the earth, observe what comes up for you and then release it. Let it go. All of your attention is here in the present. Right here. Right now. Take a couple deep breaths in slowly through your nose for the count of five and then exhale out through your mouth for the count of seven. Take your time and enjoy these moments. You are rebuilding your relationship with your body. Thank your body for everything it does for you. From the top of your head to the tips of your fingers and toes, your body is your vehicle to move upon this earth. Just as you charge your electronic devices, bringing your awareness fully into the present moment recharges your body. When you are running low on energy, you are a low battery that threatens shutting down applications and non-vital systems. Just as you bring a hostess a gift when you visit her house, give your body the gift of your desire to reconnect.

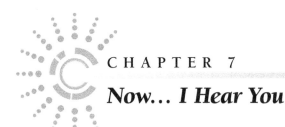

CHAPTER 7
Now… I Hear You

"People may hear your words, but they feel your attitude."
– John C. Maxwell

When Lauren and I met a couple weeks later, I could see how much her practicing being present was working for her. The lines on her face had softened, her body moved more slowly and smoothly. When we first met her body language was uptight, rigid; now she is more languid. She chooses a different chair to sit in today as well, my soft brown leather club chair, the one that feels like butter to the touch and which allows her to melt into our session.

"What would you like to receive some coaching on today?" I begin as I observe her smiling softly.

"Well, first I would like to thank you for teaching me the awareness exercise. Already things are changing for me and I couldn't be more grateful."

"What is changing for you?" I ask curiously.

"For one, my husband and I have had a couple really good conversations. We were able to talk about what has been going on with me and he actually thanked me for listening to him!"

"That's wonderful! What else is changing for you?"

"I have begun to notice things at work that I am surprised I never noticed before. It is like you said about going 100 miles an hour; how much is missed. Yesterday I noticed my assistant had a bunch of flowers on her desk. I asked who had given her such a beautiful bouquet. She told me that her boyfriend had for their one-year anniversary. Quite frankly, I didn't even know she was seeing anyone! Turns out, he has come in multiple times over the past year and I had been introduced to him on a couple of occasions. Man, I must have really been working at hyper speed to not remember him whatsoever!"

"What about your awareness moves you?"

Lauren takes a deep breath and sighs.

"I guess I feel quite a bit out of it. I had no idea how out of touch I was with the people around me, the people closest to me. It feels like I was hit over the head with a two-by-four. I am a bit dazed and yet clear."

"What have you been learning about yourself and others during this time?" Lauren's eyes widened slightly, and her face froze for a moment before it released and softened again. "I am learning that I still have some things to learn, and that hasn't been an easy pill for me to swallow." I smile knowingly. Her hard shell is beginning to soften, I think it is time to introduce the next step.

The second part of CHAT is following the thread of sensations that keeps you from knowing the truth of who you are. You do this first by being in touch with your body, by opening a dialogue with it as you turn your attention to it. Just like quantum physics double slit experiment, your awareness enables you to shift your focus from a wave of consciousness to focused choice. From here you are able to begin examining different beliefs and perspectives that are on auto pilot in your life. It is as though you are standing in a store that sells glasses. You select different pairs and place them on your face one at a time. You make notice of how they fit, feel on your face, the bridge of your nose, over your ears. You make a mental note of whether they are heavy or light, too big or too small for your face, as well as what shape and color lenses you are seeing through. There is no judgement about the glasses. What one pair may look and feel great for you, may look and feel uncomfortable for someone else. Even if identical twins were to try on glasses, they may choose differing pairs simply because one pair feels differently to the other. Your beliefs and perspectives are the same. Each of us is unique, so your beliefs and perspectives will be unique unto yourself.

As you slow your mind and become more present in each moment, you are privy to doorways, opportunities to explore yourself at a deeper level. Much like traveling along a highway, these doorways are the exits you choose to rest and nourish your body, or simply to explore what is going on along the side of the bustling road. Highway exits are clearly marked by large signs and often have smaller signs indicating what sort of services are available. Your body too, utilizes a similar system and in doing so, you are offered opportunities to explore, rest and become nourished along your journey through life.

Exercise: Sensations and Memories

I would like you to take a moment and ground yourself fully right where you are. Bring your awareness into your body by checking in with it. If you are sitting, what does the chair or ground feel like in your sit bones? Bring your awareness there. Feel into both feet by placing them firmly on the ground. Bring your awareness to your breath. Breathe in through your nose to the count of five and out through your mouth to the count of seven. Allow your body to settle and soften. Allow your body to pause. As you do this, I would like to invite you to feel into your body. What sensations are you noticing? Where in your body do you feel good? Where in your body do you feel tightness or pain? There is nothing to do with these areas, just notice and breathe. In a moment, I will be inviting you to go a little deeper into these areas and begin a dialogue with your body. Much like the conversation we have with a close friend after a period of not speaking, you want to gently reconnect. Take another deep breath in and out and then choose an area of your body to place your attention upon. If you have tight shoulders, you may place your attention on them and then witness them slowly release. You might be called to cross your arms over your chest and use your hands to massage your shoulders gently. First witness by bringing your awareness to the area that is calling your attention, and then respond to it by giving it what you feel it needs. When you are done, move onto the next area, continuing until all the areas of your body calling for your attention are feeling at ease and noticed.

"I am curious. What does it mean to be a good boss to you?"

Lauren thinks for a moment and replies, "I always imagined a good boss was someone who led the charge on the battlefield, sword outstretched in their hand, ready to conquer the enemy."

"What about this war reference relates to business for you?"

Lauren looks stunned for a moment as if she is thinking, 'War? Who said anything about war?' I wait patiently and watch her take in the metaphor.

"I suppose work, especially in sales, is about competition, conquering, taking a stand, and marking my claim on a territory."

"Interesting," I reply. "What does that boss on the battlefield look like to you?"

Lauren replies, "He looks strong but also a bit battle weary. He is dirty and bloody from the battles he is fighting, but he is committed to taking a strong stand for what he wants to conquer."

"Let's stand up and really embody this together."

I invite Lauren to stand up and I mirror her, legs in defensive T-stance, body forward, and arm outstretched. It reminds me of warrior pose in yoga, and I smile inwardly at the dichotomy of the image of war and peace I have imagined.

"What is present for you in this stance?" I ask Lauren and she makes a fierce and angry look appear on her face. Her body tenses as she holds the pose.

"I imagine my father on the battlefield in Vietnam. Although he didn't talk much about the war, I have seen enough movies to get an idea of what he went through. I imagine him leading his men and conquering land to allow his troops to advance."

"What is present in your body in this stance"

"I feel strong and capable, ready to attack whatever comes my way. I feel so strong that I might even go out and find something to attack!" She lets loose an evil laugh. "What is present in that evil laugh?"

She moves her body back to center and looks at me.

"Evil? It isn't evil. Conquering someone isn't evil, it is what needs to happen to get things done. If there were no conquering in the world, there would be no order. Everything would be chaos."

I return to center as well and watch as she speaks and then wait a moment to see if her lessons in presence kick in and what she learns from it. Her face drops and then she says, "Oh..." I remain silent and witness the wheels in her impressive mind begin to shift. "That is what I do. I conquer people."

"What is it like to conquer people?" I ask.

She thinks for several moments, her realization shifting, changing her perspective and questioning her beliefs about being a boss. "I hadn't realized I have been conquering people. I thought I was just getting people to do what I want because it was in their best interest. We are here to make money and I am really good at it. That is why I was asked to open the Half Moon Bay office and why I was promoted to district manager."

Her body sinks slightly at this realization and she looks shocked and sad at the same time.

"What is it like to be conquered?" I ask again, taking her deeper into this new awareness.

"Awful, I imagine. I don't like being ordered around, although

I don't mind people telling me what needs doing so long as it delivers the results needed."

"When in your life have you been conquered?" I dive deeper, easing the thick, solid walls around this belief to open further.

"When I was little. My father is adamant about structure and control. He says it is the only way to be prepared and safe. My mom always said it was because of the war, that he had changed when he returned home. We always did as he said though, it was just easier that way." Her voice trailed off and I watched as her face continued to soften. Tears threatened to spill over onto her cheeks and she reached her long thin fingers up to wipe them away before they could.

"What is present in your tears?" I ask.

"I was just thinking that is how I run my business and my family, too. I am constantly barking at my husband and kids for leaving things out, messes of toys, and dishes. It drives me insane. But now I am seeing how my exerting so much control over them could make me appear a bitch. It is no wonder they have been distancing themselves from me. I wouldn't want to be around me either!"

"What is gained from being so rigidly in control for you?"

"I just want there to be order. I want them to always be prepared and safe. I love them so much and I just can't stand the idea of losing them." Tears well up in her eyes again and she reaches for a tissue. "I really am not a big crier, but somehow I seem to always cry in our sessions. How do you do that?"

I smile. That is a comment I hear often I think to myself.

Lauren learned in today's session that she adopted her father's belief and need for control in order to feel safe and protected. His belief was shaped during his time in the military. At that time, it was likely a critical skill which led to him being able to return home to his wife and family. However, it was a belief that was running in the background of her life as well and caused her to act in unconscious ways. This can happen to all of us and it is the reason it is so important that you learn skills to bring your attention inward so you can surface these beliefs and perspective and then consciously choose whether they are something you really want running on automatic in your life. Some beliefs and perspectives once surfaced and examined will continue to be useful. Others you will recognize are not your own and can be set aside. You are empowered by your efforts to become clear and conscious in your life and greatly impact the relationships you have with everyone around you.

CHAPTER 8

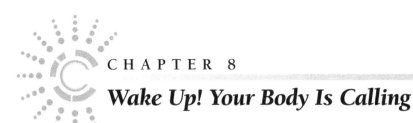

Wake Up! Your Body Is Calling

"The purpose of life is to live it, to taste experience to the utmost, to reach out eagerly and without fear for newer and richer experience."
– Eleanor Roosevelt

Over the coming weeks Lauren and I worked together, we explored her beliefs and perspectives in various areas of her life, as well as looked at the impact it was having on her various roles. With each belief and perspective, she shined the light of awareness upon herself and consciously chose which ones were true to her authentic self and the woman she aspires to be. One of the homework practices I gave to Lauren to incorporate into her life is to ground in her values each day.

Exercise: Grounding Your Values

For this exercise you will need your top five values and to be in a place where you will not be disturbed. Use the Awareness technique to get centered and grounded. Take a look at your list of values, the qualities that are most important to you. Sit quietly with your eyes closed and take each value one at a time and allow yourself to be present with it. You are welcome to slowly and softly repeat the value in your mind like a mantra, or simply envision the words floating in space before you. Whatever works for you is just fine. No judgment. Just be present. Right here. Right now.

"I am noticing that you appear much different from when I first met you Lauren. What are you noticing?"

Lauren smiles her big gorgeous grin that has become more commonplace in our sessions. "I feel different," she replies. "I feel more relaxed and happier. Things are going better at home. I am feeling a lot of love!"

"That's wonderful!" I reply, "You are very courageous to be willing to examine your beliefs and perspectives and now are experiencing the fruits of your labor." She smiles and I continue. "What would you like to receive some coaching on today?"

Lauren does not hesitate in replying, so I know this is important to her. "Although things are going really well at home, things at work could use my attention. Things are better than they were of course, but I still struggle to communicate with advisors in my district and I am hoping you can help me learn how to better connect with them."

"Why don't you tell me a little more about what you would like to learn?"

"For one, even though I don't get nearly as annoyed by my chatty Cathies at work, I still think there is more I can do to connect with them."

Ah, I think to myself, she has learned that there is a way to connect with others and still remain true to herself without competition. "What remains annoying about your chatty Cathies?"

"Even though I have slowed down quite a bit, they still like to talk. *A lot.* They are not being as efficient as they can be with their time because they focus too much on people rather than the task."

"That sounds frustrating for you. What is important for you about staying on task?"

"Getting the work done in a timely manner, getting business in the door, and making money."

"What about being task-focused helps you to get business in the door?"

Lauren thinks for a moment. She has learned that when I speak her words concisely back to her there is learning for her in the moment. I watch as she thinks about what I asked and weighs the differing perspectives in her head.

"Being task-focused is the fastest way to get from point A to B. The faster we can get to where we want to go, the more time we will have to bring in more business and therefore make more money."

"What is present for you in faster and more?"

Lauren ponders what I just said and looks like a tiger readying itself to pounce upon unsuspecting prey. "Exhilaration, the thrill of the chase!"

"What is present in your body right now when you feel into exhilaration?"

Lauren closes her eyes and feels into her body. "I feel like I am in competition and I am pushing to win the prize!"

"I can sense your excitement! Competition really gets your juices flowing, doesn't it?" Lauren nods her head as I continue, "What is present in your body right now as you feel into this exhilaration?"

She takes a deep breath and then focuses her attention within her body. "I feel tense in my shoulders and lower back. My heart is beating faster, and I can feel a rush within my veins."

"What would it be like to feel this way all of the time?" I ask. I watch as her body, once appearing as if was ready to pounce begins to soften.

"Oh no" Lauren replies, "I think I just had another a-ha moment."

What Lauren realized is the toll her competitive approach was having on her body. This was precisely the energy that caused her so many health issues not so long ago. It is a fabulous moment when you are able to feel into yourself and witness what your emotions, words, and body language are all telling you about not only what you are communicating, but also the effect it is having on your body. Being in a competitive mindset is great for short bursts of time as women, but if you remain in this state for too long, it ends up taking a toll on your health. Your adrenal glands are not built to withstand long periods of adrenaline release, and the effects of having too much cortisol running through you consistently can bring about a host of health problems from insomnia, anxiety, fatigue, weight gain, headaches, back aches, and so much more! What begins as a simple desire to feel the rush of excitement for Lauren becomes instead the trigger that releases a chain of events to occur in her body. Like dominos falling, her body switches to autopilot and initiates systems and mechanisms to go into full body protection mode. Fight or flight. It is as ancient as our ancestors, yet in our modern first-world existence is not necessary as you sit in your office or meetings in the board room. Although the same effects happen for men, their bodies are conditioned to handle these rushes of adrenaline. In fact, many men are conditioned to this release as evidenced by athletes. Even then however, if their adrenal system is not properly reset, men too can begin suffering a breakdown of their system, increased inflammation and injury often follow. A car going 100 miles an hour can only go so far before it runs out of gas. Whether you have a five-gallon or a twenty-gallon tank will determine how far you can go before you need to fill up again.

Exercise: Feeling into the Moment

The next time you feel a strong emotion, I invite you to take a breath and pause for a moment and simply tune into your body. Do not talk, just listen. What is happening in your body? Witness it with your full attention. Take notice of the effect it is having within you.

"What happens at work when you tell your chatty Cathy people what to do?"

Lauren looks at me oddly as if asked a foolish question. "They either do it or they don't. If they don't, they likely won't last very long." she replies proudly.

"Your boss told you to learn how to communicate with the advisors in your district or you'd be let go. You are still working for him. What is different about the way he conveyed this message to you?"

Lauren takes in what I say deeply and consciously. "I produce results, even though it hasn't been very good for a while, my district is at least no longer trending down."

"What does your boss do with you that is different than what you do with your advisors?"

She thinks for a moment. "Now that I think about it, he laid out a corporate strategy and provided me a framework to meet our goals to be successful."

Ah, I think. I wonder if she caught that.

"He told you what needed doing and then let you do it?" I reply back to her.

She nods her head and looks at me quizzically.

"He didn't ask you what you needed to do or micromanage your way of doing it?"

"No." I watch as another light bulb goes off for Lauren and she smiles a Cheshire cat grin.

"Ah, I see. I have been so focused on telling my people what to do that I haven't been listening to what they need to get it done. In my eagerness to get more business in the door faster I haven't taken the time to get my people on board with my plan."

"What characteristics does your boss share with your image of an ideal leader?"

Lauren thinks for a several moments and then says, "In a lot of ways he is an ideal leader. He is in the trenches with me, leads me strongly over hill and dale, gets dirty and bloody when he needs to and is a clear leader showing me the way as well."

"What comes up for you when you imagine your boss leading you this way?" "I actually feel a great deal of respect for him. I get the sense that he has my back and will do whatever it takes to get me to our goal."

"What is present in your body as you think of him in this way?"

Lauren closes her eyes and takes a moment to feel into herself. "I feel relaxed and at ease, like everything will be okay."

"What else?" Lauren feels into her body more.

"I feel calm. I am noticing that I am taking long, deep breaths rather than shallow ones. I am noticing the fragrant smell of the flowers on the table, the sound of the clock ticking on the wall."

"What would it be like to feel this way all the time?"

"Amazing."

Lauren smiles and I smile too.

Two things occurred in this session with Lauren: first, she experienced how being in competition shows up in her by bringing her awareness into her body. She also experienced how her needs when incorporated in the solution allows her to lean in and feel into a relaxed state. This is an important aspect that I work with clients around. Learning their own preferred method of communicating as well as the most productive method in which to speak to others is important as some people work best when they are told what to do, while others prefer to be asked and included in the planning. There is nothing wrong inherently with either manner, but what *is* important is knowing when to ask and when to tell. This will have a noticeable impact on your relationships at work and your personal life. Although there are no hard and fast rules in this area, here are some general guidelines in which you can experiment with people you in your life:

Prefers to be asked

- Collaborators and Researchers
- Are generally more introverted in nature (although not necessarily shy)
- Prefer to take time to do things, whether it is to get to know more about you or the situation

Prefers being told

- Leaders and Spokespersons
- Are generally more extroverted in nature
- Prefer to take action and are goal oriented whether they are focusing on work or fun

Focused on people

- Spokespersons and Collaborators
- Are concerned about the individuals involved
- Have a desire to connect and entertain
- Are generally more interested in making things enjoyable

Focused on task

- Leaders and Researchers
- Are concerned with what needs to get done
- Have a desire to produce results or learn more about things
- Are generally interested in getting things done or figuring out why

Understanding how others communicate and what role they play in life will enable you to better work as a team. Knowing this information can greatly accelerate your learning and catapult you into your projected future faster and more easily. Along your journey, you will become aware of the many gifts of understanding you are privy to. The more understanding you have, the more genteel and civilized your world becomes. We all have a learning curve in life. The faster you can grasp what you need to know, the more enjoyable your journey becomes, and less challenges you suffer with more peace you feel. Many are awaiting the coming of a savior, a superhero of sorts who brings peace and abundance back to our world. It is time you fully embody your internal superhero and get to have more fun while doing it!

Inquiry:

What comes up for you around what you just read? What are some examples of these types of people in your life? What does understanding their role help you to let go of in your life? The heat of awareness is much like traveling from somewhere cold to someplace warm. It is time to lighten your load and leave any unneeded baggage behind as we start your journey home. Knowing your core type as well as the role you are playing are key to not getting lost in character, unable to remove the costume you are wearing and move onto other roles in other plays. Knowing your type is understanding the role you have come here to act out on the stage of life. Sometimes you may be the main character, sometimes a supporting character. No matter your role, every job is important to the success of the play.

Life is a series of plays and we are all actors on this one great stage. Sometimes you get to wear brilliant costumes that make the play shine. Other times you are wearing costumes that are grey and dismal, acting out a tragedy instead. Understanding that all plays come to an end, you can let go of the role you played and move onto something else. You create baggage when you try to carry those old, worn-out costumes that are too small for you, too tight and tattered to serve your roles in future plays. Creating a healthy relationship with yourself is the best way to make this happen.

CHAPTER 9
Aligning Heart with Body Wisdom

"As our heart summons our strength, our wisdom must direct it."
– Dwight D. Eisenhower

"What has been your biggest takeaway so far in our coaching?" I ask Lauren a few weeks later when we meet.

"I think the awareness I have gained. Between learning to slow down and be present and in noticing what is happening in my body and the impact I have on other people, I feel like I am transforming into a better version of me." She smiles her gorgeous grin relaxing back into my soft brown leather chair.

"Tell me, what would you like to receive some coaching on today?"

Lauren thinks awhile and asks, "I am not sure. You work with other leaders like me, so I bet you have quite a few tools in your tool belt."

I nod my head, smile at her and say, "It is quite the change I am witnessing in you. I knew you were driven and successful when I met you, strong and capable. I have since witnessed you as courageous and heartfelt. There are some other tools I can share. These agreements have helped many women develop healthy relationships with themselves and others. They were created by Awakening Women and are helpful to anyone who is ready to step fully into a heart-centered life. I'll give you a copy of them when you leave, but we can go over them briefly now if you would like?

That way you can ask any questions you may have, although they are pretty straightforward."

"I would really appreciate that, thank you!" Lauren replies.

AWAKENING WOMEN
SISTERHOOD MANIFESTO

I commit to be honest and direct with you

I commit to take responsibility for myself

I will ask for support when I need it

I will ask for alone time when I need it, and it means nothing personal to you

I will not try to fix you

I will listen to you

I will keep what you share confidential and not gossip about it

I will not speak negatively about you to others

I will celebrate your unique beauty and gifts

I will not hold myself back to fit in and I will support you in doing the same

After Lauren and I had a chance to go over the agreements, I asked her what she thought of them and how they could be put into action in her life.

"They all sound good, but just because I follow these guidelines doesn't mean anyone else will."

"Fair point." I reply, "These guidelines are manners in which you can live your life fully and wholly. There will be people who don't adhere to them just as there are people who don't adhere to the laws of our society. You have done an incredible job in becoming less rigid in your structure, and some structure is healthy for your life. Structure is the riverbank that directs the water flow in a river. Without the structure of the riverbank, the water would pour out everywhere and the river would become drained. With structure, the river can flow easily even around rocks, logs and other obstacles that get in the way. It is the same with the masculine and feminine qualities within us that we discussed when we first started working together. The more you are in alignment and rest into the cycles that occur in your projects or goals, the easier it becomes to manage different stages in your life. Much like the waves of the ocean crashing and retreating from the shore, there is rhythm to what you do.

Inquiry:

Get centered and grounded by using the Awareness technique. After you have taken your deep inhales in for five counts and exhales out for seven counts, I would like you to close your eyes and consider where expansion and contraction are showing up in your life right now. Breathe into this exercise and pay attention to the expansion and contraction in your body as you bring each memory one by one into the present moment. What do you notice in your body as each memory comes to mind? Do you notice heaviness or lightness? Observe what your body wisdom is sharing with you. What was the outcome of the situation? What emotion rises within you at the memory?

I invite Lauren to do this inquiry with me at our next session.

"Tell me Lauren, where are you experiencing expansion and contraction in your life right now?"

Lauren thinks a few moments and replies, "I am noticing the relationships with my family seem to be expanding. Relationships I have at work seem to be contracting although they have gotten much better."

"What is present in the expansion with your family?" I ask.

"It just seems like we are all getting along better and having a lot more fun than we used to."

"What one emotion would you attribute to the state of your family relationships right now?"

Lauren hesitates only a moment before replying, "Love."

"What is present in the contraction with work?" I ask Lauren.

"I have utilized the tools you have given me so far and that has made a huge difference at work. I just feel like we haven't gotten things completely dialed in just yet." "What does it feel like in your body when you think about things not being completely dialed in yet?" I inquire as I watch Lauren begin to shift her body in her chair.

"I feel uncomfortable, like things are tight."

"What is tight about work for you right now?"

"We have an internal audit coming up and are nearing quarter end, that always gets me feeling on edge."

Lauren says as she rolls her eyes and I nod in agreement.

"Even though I think I have been connecting better with my advisors and managers, they still don't do what I tell them to do – even with all of your suggestions on how to communicate with them."

"Interesting," I say to Lauren. "What do you imagine is the cause of this?"

"I am not sure, other than I am feeling more stressed lately."

"Where is the stress showing up in your body?"

"All the typical places, my neck, and my lower back."

"What do your neck and lower back do for your body?"

"My neck supports my head I guess. My lower back supports my spine."

"So where are you not receiving support at work?"

Lauren's eyes flash wide open at my words and she replies, "I haven't been getting the funding necessary for the budget that I need to hire additional support staff since my district is in third to last place."

When you tune into your body and listen to the wisdom it

shares, you gain essential information to guide your life. Not every time you tune in and listen will it be as clear as it is for Lauren, but follow that thread inward and you will expose beliefs and perspectives you have that can be causing your body wisdom to send off warning signals of things that require your attention.

"When you feel into your lower back and neck pain, what comes up for you?"

"The lack of support of course, but it feels like there is something else going on too. When I imagine my back and neck, I see them getting tight and rigid."

"Where in your work life are you tight and rigid?" I say to Lauren.

"I am a bit worried about my standing in the nation. If my district doesn't show a clear turnaround, I may lose my job."

"What has changed with your advisors in this lack of support you are feeling?"

Lauren thinks a few moments and then declares, "Nothing. They are all responding much better to my direction now that I speak their language."

"What has changed in your environment in this lack of support you are feeling?"

"Nothing has changed."

"What *has* changed in this lack of support you are feeling?"

Lauren remains quiet for quite a long time. I wait patiently for her to work through her thoughts. "I am the only thing that seems to have changed."

"Interesting observation," I reply. "What is it about you that has changed?" I invite Lauren to observe.

"I have become more stressed out about the audit and the upcoming quarter end." "What one emotion would you attribute to these feelings of being stressed out?" Lauren hesitates then replies, "Fear."

Love and fear are prime motivators in life. When you make decisions based on these primal emotions, you experience the effects playing out in your body. Even if you make a decision from a place of love, your beliefs and perspectives can often act like a kaleidoscope interfering with your intention being clear and focused. Once your beliefs and perspectives are consciously chosen, you stand a much better chance of being clear about the source from which you project your life forward.

Inquiry:

Think of a decision you need to make. It could be big or small, but really feel into each choice you have. One that is rooted in fear will often create heaviness, tightness, qualities of contraction in your body. A choice that is rooted in love will often create lightness, expansive qualities that are associated with ease. When you tune in and follow the thread that leads to the basis of your decision, you empower your ability to trust yourself and make conscious decisions which are in alignment for you.

Lauren feels into her body and realizes the choices she makes are mostly rooted in fear. She fears that she could lose her job if her district doesn't pass audit, or worse if it does not rate higher when compared to the rest of the districts in the nation. When she changes her focus to that of openness by considering how they have a structure in place to secure a pass on the audit and the success of her communication skills with her team, she feels a release in her lower back and neck. She feels lighter, more expansive and she experiences a new way of thinking about her plan for the district.

When you are clear and rooted in the experience of expansion and abundance, your decisions become clear and the road to achieve successful fulfillment of your goals becomes focused and direct. No longer in a flight or fight response, the lighter feelings of ease and flow allow your body to restore and heal. From this place of clarity and ease, you allow new ideas to show up and create opportunities to achieve your desired results with ease.

CHAPTER 10

Getting Things Done without Burning Out

"Life is too short for shoes to hurt your feet,
friends that make you feel bad about yourself,
and jobs that crush your soul. Take a chance.
Make a change. The time is now."
– Lisa Lewton

In the previous chapters you learned about the first two parts of CHAT: conscious awareness by examining any beliefs and perspectives on autopilot in your body, then choosing the ones you want to keep going forward. This can take anywhere from a little to a long time, depending how much you are willing to reset your body wisdom and rely on the information it provides you. Lauren is ready for the third step in CHAT. Having learned she can rebuild a foundation of beliefs and perspectives which serve her in meeting successful fulfillment of her goals in a healthy, empowering way, she now is able to bring her wisdom to the surface and utilize the gifts she has uncovered to realize the results she wants to achieve. I coach Lauren on ways of tapping into her body wisdom, as well as getting grounded and clear so she gets results.

"What would you like to receive some coaching on today?" I ask Lauren who is looking healthier and more relaxed than I have ever seen her before.

"How do I know that the messages I am getting from my body

are ones I can trust?" Lauren looked pleadingly with her eyes. "What have you learned from tapping into your body wisdom so far?" I inquire.

"I have learned that my body gives me clues to whether something feels right or wrong to me. I have learned that my body knows things even before I do in my mind."

"What experiences have led you to the portal that is present right now?"

Lauren details some experiences she has had lately that have helped her communicate more effectively with her advisors, family and health.

"What about these experiences do you still not trust?" I ask when she is through.

"I guess I have quite a bit of evidence to support that I am on the right track." She replies sheepishly. "I just want to be able to trust that my employees will meet the goals I have given them so I can reach my goal of being a top producing office."

"What do you gain from having control over others ability to get their work done?" Lauren looks at me a bit shocked and answers, "The confidence in knowing the job was done correctly and the assurance of realizing my desired outcome."

"When you feel into your body, where do you experience feelings of control?"

Lauren closes her eyes and feels into her body. "I imagine a large knot in the pit of my stomach."

"Tell me about the large knot in your stomach? What size, color, and shape is it?" Lauren takes a deep breath and focuses her awareness on the knot.

"It is about the size of a medium sized ball, is hard, twisted and gray. Oddly, the shape is more of butternut squash rather than round."

"Interesting observation," I said, "What about the butternut squash shape surprises you?"

"For one, butternut squash reminds me of fall. When leaves change colors, the air becomes crisp and cool. Fall is the time that leaves fall to the ground and I begin putting things away at the house as I prepare for winter."

"What needs to be let go in your life so you can prepare for the next stage?"

Lauren thought about that for some time and tuned into her body to verify she was on the right track by following the feelings of lightness, flow, and ease.

"I am realizing I need to let go of control over everyone and everything. I need to trust that I have hired the right people and let them do their work toward the goals and objectives I have laid out for them."

Many times when you feel the need to control yourself or your environment, there is fear present. What's more, it is the driving force behind the belief system that is running your life in the background. The emotion of fear and whatever belief it joins hands with, take over all aspects of your life like cancer cells invading your body. On a deep level, fear wants to protect you. It is the part of yourself that is unaware of your current environment or situation and makes decisions based upon a very small aspect of knowledge and history of experiences of you. Many times when you have thoughts of fear, worry or concern, these thoughts do not serve you and are like a broken record on repeat in your brain, "I can't do that," "That will hurt," "If I try that then I could fail." Below is the method I taught Lauren and many of my clients so they could regain trust and remove irrational thoughts or fears that continue to plague them.

Exercise: Grounding and Observing

Follow the Awareness Technique to get fully present in your body. As you sit with your feet firmly rooted in the ground beneath you, imagine a cord or chain dropping from the center of your hips directly down to the center of the earth. Imagine this cord or chain moves effortlessly through each layer of rock, sand and dirt, down into the liquid magna at our earth's core. Imagine there is a hook at the end of the cord or chain and imagine attaching it securely to the earth's core. Follow the cord or chain back up to where it attaches to your body and imagine flipping a light switch which opens a portal for all the unwanted and no longer needed items in your life to flow easily into the earth like water flowing down a drain. Imagine there is a large bubble around you. It could be far out in front of you or held more closely around your body. Wherever it is, just notice it for a moment. This bubble is flexible and can expand and contract easily merely by your thought of it doing so. Take a few moments to play with this bubble, expanding it outward and inward until it is comfortable for you, about eighteen inches around your body is good. Take a look around the inside of the bubble. If there is anything you do not want here, let it go down your grounding cord into the earth. People, situations, thoughts, emotions all can be released down the grounding cord where the earth will transmute those thoughts and feelings easily and effortlessly like a plant converts carbon dioxide into oxygen. Breathe and release. Let everything go, just breathe.

Next, place your attention in the area just behind your eyes. Imagine there is a room in this place, a space that is all your own. No one knows of this place or can access this place except you; only you have the power to invite others inside. For now, ask anyone who is in this room to leave. This is your home, the place of self. The room is small, just big enough for a place to sit and a large television screen and a few items that comfort you. Take a look around the room and observe what it looks like. You can take a few moments to make yourself comfortable, adjust the temperature in the room or tidy up a bit. Do whatever it takes to make this room fully your own.

When you are ready, sit down facing the television screen and bring your attention to the black screen in front of you. Breathe. On the screen in front of you, imagine a rose. Take your time as you imagine the rose. If you can't imagine it, just pretend you can. You may see it, or smell it, or maybe you just know the rose is there. However you sense the rose, bring your attention fully upon it. Imagine the soft petals and the stem. What color is your rose? What does it look like? Is it a tight bud? Fully open? Or somewhere in between? Does the rose have thorns? If so, are they large or small? Many or few? Take your time and just breathe. There is no right or wrong answer here. It is all observation and only you will know the answer. Allow your attention to focus on the rose, every detail as clear as you can get it. Breathe. Now I would like you to imagine there is a stick of dynamite at the base of the rose and watch as it blows the rose up into millions of tiny pieces that evaporate into the screen. Breathe. What is happening in your body right now? Notice what comes up and then just let those thoughts go, easily, effortlessly, like water going down a drain. Continue playing by imagining another rose and bringing your awareness fully to it, observing what it looks, feels, smells like, then blow it up as well. Keep doing this as many times as you like. The more comfortable you become, the easier this happens outside of this inward state. Continue breathing and when you are ready, open your eyes.

We are incredible creators and this last exercise allows you to experience destroying as well. The rose is any thought you have. No matter how you sense it, or whether you just had to pretend it was there, the image of the rose enables you to see your thought and then change it simply by bringing you awareness to it. You can do the same with any belief or perspective you have or even emotions you are feeling. Imagine whatever you are feeling and allow it to be poured out of you and into the rose you create then simply blow it up. Each moment you breathe is a moment you are creating thoughts. When you feel cluttered and unclear with too many thoughts filling up your head, use this exercise to "blow up" anything you no longer want or need. Think of it like a paper shredder and the old thought files getting released. In doing this, you enable the powerful aspects of yourself to come forward and consciously choose the best way to get the results you want with less effort and more ease.

Exercise

Write a list of beliefs that you have told yourself over your lifetime that are no longer serving you and then use the Grounding and Observing technique to blow them up.

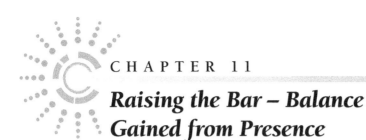

CHAPTER 11
Raising the Bar – Balance Gained from Presence

"Presence is more than just being there."
– Malcomb Forbes

I taught Lauren the grounding and observing technique and showed her how she could apply it to her life when she has thoughts that are not in alignment with her goals.

"What are you thinking now that isn't aligned with a goal you have?" I ask Lauren as the warm sun pours in through the window near us.

"There is one office in my district I am struggling to get on board with the plan I have to make my district a top performer. The manager and I don't see eye to eye, but my boss has let me know that he's not going anywhere so I need to figure out how to make this work."

"Tell me more about the challenges you are having with him." I say. "He is quite stubborn and fixed in his thinking. He thinks he knows everything and can do whatever he wants…"

I interrupt Lauren and remind her that is a perspective she has on him, rather than who he is necessarily.

"Tell me his attributes. Have you figured out his personality type yet?" I inquire. "No, I haven't. I forgot about doing that." Lauren smiles and giggles remembering that she has a tool for this. "He is very well educated and is pretty quiet. He is always referring to articles he's read or the latest financial news. He sends out very well researched and thought out newsletters to the clients in his office."

I interrupt Lauren again and ask if she has figured out his type.

"I think so. Is he a Researcher?"

I smile and reply, "You tell me. You have adjectives that describe him as well as a method to check your body wisdom to see if you are correct."

Lauren pauses for a moment and feels into herself. She feels light and calm and she answers, "He is a Researcher. Now I remember that Researchers are analytical and don't like to be told what to do. They want evidence to support what I am directing them to do."

"You are resourceful and intuitive! You used your gifts to have confidence in your choice. What are some things you can do to connect with him?"

Lauren thinks for a few moments and yells out, "Oh! I could send him a link to that article I read recently that speaks of the method I am using to meet our goals. It is not written for a district manager of course, but he is smart enough to relate the conclusions to my desired results."

"How would you describe this manager with your awareness now?"

Lauren smiles and says, "I no longer think he is stubborn, but rather needs more evidence to get his buy in before he adopts my plan. He may still be fixed minded, but if I present him with supporting evidence, it will compel him to get on board. I am also remembering that he has multiple degrees including a graduate degree, as well as his CFP and CMA, so he has a lot of education as well as experience."

"Great observation and knowing. What other things are getting in the way of fostering a great connection with him?"

Lauren pauses and looks up and to her left. I know now that

she stores her memories by visualizing them. A look up and to the right generally indicates someone is remembering what was said or the sounds from their memory. Both of these, when linked to the emotion you feel at that moment in the memory, is what you can bring your awareness to and help melt the hold a belief or idea has on your thinking. You are able to bring conscious awareness and choose the direction you want to go.

"I don't know why I keep thinking this but, he reminds me of my uncle." Lauren answers.

"Tell me about your uncle? What are your first thoughts of him?"

Lauren doesn't hesitate in her reply, "He is stubborn, challenging for anyone in the family to deal with. I loved his parents – both are so inclusive and friendly! They tried so hard to create a relationship with him, but he is just too damn reserved and angry. 'Everything is a fight with him' is what my aunt and uncle used to tell my mom."

I nod my head to acknowledge I am listening and then say, "What is his personality type I wonder…." I let my voice trail off and await Lauren's reply.

"He is a Researcher."

"What personality type do you think his parents are?" I pose to her.

"Since they are inclusive and friendly and all about relationships, I would say they are Collaborators." Lauren thinks for a moment about their situation and the knowledge she now possesses. "So the reason they always had problems with him is because they expected him to get on board with what they said, their plans, and parenting, What he needed was for them to provide compelling evidence that what they were telling him was the best way to go about accomplishing his goals. I wonder if reaching out to him in this way would improve their relationship with him?"

"What does your body tell you?" Lauren feels into her body and struggles to identify what she is feeling. "I am feeling all sorts of things. Lightness. Heaviness. Slightly nauseous, wide awake."

I recognize these experiences and guide Lauren to ground herself with a modified version of the Grounding and Observing technique and we continue.

"When you bring your awareness to the space right behind your eyes and get settled into the room you have created, your safe space, I want you to create and destroy a few roses."

Lauren signals to me when she is done, and I continue leading her through the exercise.

"Now I would like you to watch the screen and observe what happens when I say the word '*yes*.'"

Lauren reports she sees a green light and feels a quick surge of excitement.

I continue, "Now the same thing with the word '*no*.' What do you notice?"

Lauren reports she sees a red light and feels the presence of a wall before her. I ask her one more time about the word "*perhaps*" and she reports seeing a yellow light and feeling nothing. I take her through the exercise a couple more times until she feels really clear about the image and feeling she experiences at each word. I continue, "Now I would like you to ask yourself quietly without speaking, if your name is Lauren." She does and gets a green light and associated feeling. I ask her a couple more questions that she knows the answers to as well as one I know she would be unsure about. To each question she received associated light, colors and feelings. "Now ask any questions one by one you have about your cousin or his parents and observe what answers you get. Keep in mind to ask simple yes, no, maybe questions and also to ask your question multiple ways if you want to be certain of the information you receive". Lauren sits quietly and I patiently wait for her to surface with the information she has uncovered. Sitting with her eyes still closed, she answers at last, "I am really clear about the situation with my relatives and I actually had a big a-ha about my Researcher manager!"

"You are patient and resourceful with the tools you have learned! What will you do with this new awareness?"

Lauren thinks a moment and then states, "Nothing. I have a sense of what this manager needs and how I can approach him, so he gets on board with my plan for the district. I feel confident that I can connect with him and in fact, have the sense that he will become my biggest ally in the process!"

Lauren looks amused and excited and when she opens her eyes, I notice a tear threatening to ease from the corner of her eye down her nose.

"What is in that tear?" I ask with compassion.

"I am so happy! I cannot tell you how much your coaching has given me over the past few months! When I look back at the time before we started, I hardly recognize the old me."

"What is the biggest takeaway from sessions together?"

"That I really can get better results with a lot less effort when I use the wisdom of my mind, heart *and* body!"

We smile at each other and I nod my head knowingly.

"You've got this Lauren! I have confidence that you now have the tools it takes to live your best life yet!"

I wrapped up our last coaching session together by going over her life map and asked her what her top five values were now. Lauren realized every area of her life had improved and she was feeling calm and happy. She now has multiple tools to connect with others and herself and is leaving empowered to create the work relationships that help her reach her goals. Her quarter end came, and her district had moved up nine spots and she was feeling certain she could get to the top three by year end now that she had developed a good relationship with her Researcher type manager. She told me she knew it could happen because she saw a green light and felt that sudden surge of excitement when she checked in with her body. I too see it happening for her and you as well. By deepening the relationship with every aspect of ourselves, we activate every tool we have and create a life of our own making. You cease to be a victim to your life but rather take your place as creator and make your choices consciously and without the unnecessary interference of your lizard brain.

CHAPTER 12

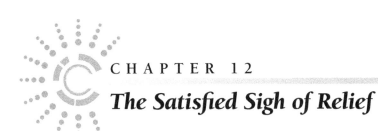

The Satisfied Sigh of Relief

"The body says what words cannot."
– Martha Graham

Lauren came to coaching because she wasn't getting the results she wanted at work. She also stated during our first session that she was experiencing health issues and struggles with her family. She could have consulted any number of coaches and she would likely have made some progress with them. She and my clients have learned that the work we do together creates lasting change as you learn tools that are easy for you to incorporate in your daily life, as you gain clarity and experience more ease and flow.

Inquiry:

- What is holding you back from living this moment to the fullest?
- What is holding you back from the life available to you right now?
- What is the cost of choosing not to examine your beliefs and choose ones that are in alignment with who you are?
- What is the cost to your relationships, your work, and personal lives? What is the toll it is taking on your health?

Now that you have examined the cost, I would like you to consider the benefit gained for each area of your life. If I were to wave a magic wand, what would be possible for you?

These methods will work for anyone who has an open mind and is courageous enough to shine the light of awareness upon themselves rather than placing the blame of their troubles on everyone around them. Courage to look inward is what builds character and becomes the riverbanks that direct the course and flow your life takes. Creating a strong and healthy relationship with yourself is the key to experiencing strong and healthy relationships with others. Be the change you want to see in the world and watch as your world changes.

Many of the clients I have taught CHAT to have gone on to elevate their lives and experience successful results while enjoying their work and rest of their life. There are even some who have gone on and developed their own tools, adopting other ways to connect with themselves and integrated various esoteric methods to improve their communication skills so they speak in ways which are easy for others to listen and listen in ways that allow others to feel heard.

There are multiple techniques available to you, but these listed in the previous chapters have been proven to work as reported by the transformations my clients and people around me have made. The agreements made in the sisterhood manifesto further form the foundation for your best life and become the cornerstones of getting the results you desire. These agreements are not only for women, but men too can embrace these agreements and also honor the women in their lives by following them. Combining masculine and feminine elements (structure and freedom) in a balanced way that is aligned with your body, adding in understanding of who you are in relationship with others, as well as communication methods, personality types and intuition you now know, suddenly makes you a powerful force to live your best life yet!

Inquiry:

I would like you to take a moment and consider this question,
"I need _______ so I can_________ for myself"

What do you need? What will that enable you to do? Then ask the same question for others – your work, partner, children, family, friends. Tune into your body wisdom and observe what answers you get. This exercise is a portal into what is holding you back from realizing your goals.

One last thing I would like to share are the results of many studies completed to examine the benefits of gratitude in our body mind. One study conducted by Dr. Robert Emmons, UC Davis, and Dr. Michael McCullough, University of Miami, describes how gratitude physically rewires the brain much like neural pathways rewire habits. Give your gratitude journal twenty-one days, the length of time it takes for new neural pathways to be created and old ones destroyed. The people in the study who did this experienced feeling more optimistic and positive, as well as having reported fewer visits to the doctor than the group who wrote negative comments. Focusing on the positive can also improve sleep quality and reduce feelings of anxiety and depression, giving you better moods, less fatigue and reducing overall stress and the health conditions stress can create. In addition, a quick google search of "gratitude rewires your brain" will list a number of other studies conducted and prove further the effect of gratitude in our lives. This is important as the more grateful we become for what we have and what we have learned, the more ease and flow occurs in our life, the more challenges get averted with quick, clear thinking and body wisdom.

Exercise

Get a journal that you can carry with you or create a special note file on your phone that allows you to keep a log of people and situations you are grateful for each day. You may start out with little or big items, the sunny, warm day or even waking up and seeing, smelling, tasting, touching, hearing the world around you. Write five things down for twenty-one days in your gratitude journal even as you apply the techniques and tools learned in this book. I promise you will be grateful that you did.

You have now reached the end of this book. I hope you have found it useful and are realizing the results you want in your work and personal life.

As a review, here are the tools you now know and can refer to at any time:

Personality types: Leader, Spokesperson, Researcher, and Collaborator. You have learned how to identify your core type and how to identify others and whether they are coming from a conscious or unconscious state, as well as their preferred communication style and way to honor your connection.

CHAT: Conscious Heart Awareness Technique and the tools that get you grounded and centered. You have learned how to become present and conscious with yourself and your surroundings, how to examine and choose beliefs and perspectives that are uniquely aligned with who you are and what type of person you want to be. You have learned tools to bring your attention inward as well as a manner in which you can verify your intuition and create a lasting, trusting relationship with your innate body wisdom. You have learned methods that reveal how you receive insight as well as how to utilize that information so you can get results faster and with less effort. With regular implementation of these tools you will experience a life that flows more easily, by utilizing the many gifts of the masculine and feminine contained within you.

You are now empowered with gifts of wisdom our foremothers and forefathers used to navigate their lives and create relationships with their community and world around them. It is in this remembering that you recover the gifts gained throughout your life. Applying these gifts and tools with conscious awareness enables you to get really clear about where you want to go. How then becomes easy since you simply continue to listen and allow (instead of forcing) the steps to unfold. You become clear, a satellite dish recording and releasing information available within and around you each moment. This clarity reveals opportunities coming your way, as well as insight that is not readily available to you when living solely on the surface of your life.

What have you decided to do with this one life you are living? What tools did you uncover to start getting better results with less effort? What other tools can you use to connect more deeply with the people in your life? What are you going to go out and accomplish now that you have a map and all the resources you have gained to get you on your way? What are the possibilities at work? How about in your personal life? What do you want your life to be? The time has come for you to step fully into who you are and to succeed in the goals you have for your work and personal life.

Conclusion

I have used the methods I teach clients in this book to get results I want more easily and to gain clarity about the beliefs and perspectives I hold. Through my journey, I have also realized increased health and wellbeing as well as a reduction of chronic health issues. This has been so critical to living the life I want to lead that it has compelled me to teach this technique to others. I get so much pleasure watching you become empowered by making conscious choices, witnessing you realize fulfillment and happiness in your life. Helping clients like you is what gets me out of bed and never thinking about retiring. I want so much for you to experience the results you deserve at work and in all areas of your life. I want so much for you to experience healthy and supportive relationships. That is why I wrote this book, to give you the benefit of my knowledge, education and experience so you too, can realize the relationships of your dreams!

As you can tell, I am super passionate about the work I do! I enjoy writing, teaching and speaking about this technique especially in business settings. Most large companies and organizations like Apple, Microsoft, Google, Chicago Bulls, and many others have incorporated visualization or meditation techniques into their culture at leadership levels because they recognize the increased benefit to their businesses and employees. Many other companies and organizations utilize other personality tests or other descriptive measures in order to get their teams communicating with better results. This is wonderful and needed in our world, yet just about everyone stops there. What makes CHAT and the tools in this book different is the combining of multiple techniques. Your body wisdom ends up supporting you individually which enables you to become the best version of yourself without needing to step on anyone else in the process. In fact, once you learn these tools and techniques, you will often find you have more than enough time to help others around you by modeling your increased levels of happiness, joy and fulfillment in life. This, dear reader, is the peace on earth we long to experience, the life of peace and love promised to us.

Acknowledgments

I would like to thank my many teachers that have shown me their tools and techniques so I could tune into my own body, begin the process of healing and come out the other side accomplishing all the goals I have for myself with a lot less effort. I appreciate that each of them allowed me to discover my own innate gifts and are now able to integrate them into my daily life, so I live my best self each day.

I would also like to thank all the challenging people I have encountered in my life who have taught me so much not only about themselves, but also about myself.

I would like to thank my Spokesperson husband George especially. You have provided me endless support and so much love as I have taken my business to the next level. Your patience and ability to listen to my seemingly endless ideas about what I wanted to share in this book have earned you the highest honor I can bestow. I love you to the stars and back; everlasting is my love for you.

I would also like to thank my Researcher son Owen. You may never know how much I love you, or how important it has been for me to build a strong and lasting relationship with you. Thank you for challenging me and helping me to grow as a mother and human being.

Lastly, I would like to thank my Leader mother Kitty. You have given me endless gifts to become the woman I am today, and I thank you from the bottom of my heart. See you on the flip side of life!

About the Author

Teresa Lodato, CPCC, is a certified Executive Leadership & Relationship Coach and lover of people, connection, community and relationship. From a very young age she was fascinated by people of all walks of life, different cultures, languages and lifestyles left her curious and wanting to know more. She has spent her life exploring, traveling and meeting people, experiencing cultures, traditions, communities and relationships. She is curious about why people do the things they do, how their beliefs are formed and what motivates them. This worldview perspective means she is open minded and nonjudgmental. It is safe for you to bring whatever your heart desires to your sessions, in fact she asks that you do.

Throughout her life Teresa worked in male-dominated industries which gave her a great deal of insight into male and female psyches and helped form the perspectives she now holds. Over the past few years she has worked with other top relationship experts who have done extensive research from a psychological, as well as societal and personal viewpoint. It turns out their conclusions about how men and women relate are beliefs and perspectives she naturally holds through her own experience. Teresa's own studies and research came to the forefront while in graduate school studying Psychology (Counseling and Consciousness and Transformative Studies) and also during training and certification through CTI (Co-Active Training Institute). Because of her vast experience, both research- and experiential-based, Teresa is able to bring many tools to your sessions in order to assist with your Executive Leadership & Relationship Coaching needs.

Formerly a divorced woman who found love online and overcame the statistics by marrying the love of her life in her forties, she now lives in the San Francisco Bay Area with her blended family: one child from each of their marriages and another born in 2016. She enjoys hiking, yin yoga, spending time with friends, playing golf, volunteering with local animal assisted therapy groups, and serving on various boards for patient support and therapy programs. As a working mom, she has a lot to balance. The most important thing to her is keeping priorities in line and maintaining the skill set to maneuver the complexities of her modern-day love affair!

Thank You

Thank you for taking the time to read *Why Aren't You Listening to Me?* You have taken the first steps to realizing better results with less effort and learned great tools and techniques to tune into your body wisdom. My wish for you is that you continue to practice and apply what you have learned here to benefit not only your work, but the rest of your life as well.

If you are struggling with a particular area of this book, feel free to reach out to me at teresa.lodato.cpcc@gmail.com and I will help you the best I can. You are also welcomed to book a complimentary session with me by reserving time on my calendar. During that time, you can ask me any questions you have about the techniques and tools in this book or to learn more about how working with me can help you achieve extraordinary results with less effort. I also offer an eight week online course to support you in continuing your journey. Please visit my website at: www.teresalodato.com for more information or to sign up.

I would love to connect with you! Feel free to follow me on Instagram at @Teresa_Lodato_CPCC and Facebook @Teresa.Lodato.CPCC for more information and insight into creating business and personal lives that you never want to leave.

In life's journey you get to plan your stay.
Make it a good one!

CPSIA information can be obtained
at www.ICGtesting.com
Printed in the USA
LVHW112321260620
659106LV00007B/86/J